Ask The Janitor

An Insider's Look at Public School Education in America

DR. JOHN B. MUCIACCIA

D1292397

ISBN: 0974475505
ISBN 13: 9780974475509

"Education is the most powerful weapon which you can use to change the world."

Nelson Mandela
1918-2013

DEDICATION

*This book is dedicated to the many hard-working teachers in schools throughout this country;
past, present, and future. Our world is filled with wonderful men and women who have made
teaching their life's joy. As a result of their commitment, students who are fortunate enough
to study with them, develop a love of the disciplines being taught, a love that in some cases
can last a lifetime. These teachers tend to quickly become student favorites and through their
energy and enthusiasm foster an atmosphere of learning that is not soon forgotten.*

*Like many of you, I fondly remember many of my elementary, high school, and college teachers.
I think and talk about them often. They inspired me to become a teacher and, indirectly, to
write this book. Many teachers working now are of that caliber and love the work they do.*

That love is evident to their students and contagious in the most wonderful way.

*It is for the purpose of honoring these teachers and developing more like them that I write
this book. Besides the home, where else can we influence the current generation of children
more positively than in the schools they attend? Nelson Mandela said it best when he said,*

"Education is the most powerful weapon which you can use to change the world."

*It is in that spirit that this book is dedicated to the loving teachers who occupy our classrooms.
May you multiply and grow exponentially in all the great things you do. Your work is sacred
and of great importance.*

TABLE OF CONTENTS

REASON FOR THE TITLE

The title *Ask The Janitor* was inspired by the fondness I felt throughout my teaching career for the men and women who called themselves janitors. Although they were responsible for the cleanliness and maintenance of the school building, their jobs found them doing much more than mopping floors and repairing desks. In some ways, they were surrogate mothers and fathers to the students, offering counsel to those in conflict with their teachers and/or parents.

The men and women who came into my life as school janitors might have been the least formally educated people in the school system, many with only an elementary school education, but in spite of that, they demonstrated the most respect and common sense in everything they did and said.

As an unwritten rule, the janitor's room was off-limits to all but the janitors, nevertheless, I was always warmly welcomed there. They felt my respect and admiration, so they welcomed me into their inner sanctum.

As I look back, I had the habit of entering the school through the janitor's entrance located in the rear of the building near the parking lot. This janitor's entrance was to me like the stage entrance to a theatre. It was the door through which insiders entered. Students and visitors entered through the front door, along with the vast majority of teachers.

I could always count on the janitors to tell me the truth without any political sugar coating. Administrators, teachers, and even board members would often offer politically compromised answers to my queries, not so the janitors. They always gave it to me straight and, as a result, they were a breath of fresh air in the politically charged environment of the public school system.

Janitors use simple, street-knowledge to interpret and understand the workings of a school. They don't allow college degrees to get in the way of common sense. When they see a problem, they immediately start looking for practical solutions. They would never dream of forming a committee to get in the way of answers as so many of us in education do. Janitors don't skirt the clear answers they see in favor of politically convenient ones. They get the job done quickly and with the least amount of energy. Very often, they know of a problem before it becomes obvious to others in the school community. I always went to the janitors when in search of truthful information regarding a school issue and was never misled.

As a rule, janitors were older employees with a parental energy about them, and it was to this nourishing, wise energy that I was drawn. And now, it is in that energy that I honor the simple truths given to me by them. If only teachers, administrators, and board members lived by the same rule of simple truths, imagine what a wonderful world we would have within our public schools!

PREFACE

This is the story of my experiences working in the American public school system during a 32 year career both as an educator and administrator. It is told from the heart and is meant to be received not as an indictment, but as a call to attention so we can reclaim our belief in public school education.

The book is also a reflection of 44 consecutive Septembers that found me in a public school, either as a student or as an employee. School has been a large part of my life; some of my happiest memories as well as some of the saddest have been associated with a school. Likewise, the most wonderful as well as the least wonderful people I have met, I met in or through a school. My emotions, both high and low, have come from these school experiences and, as a result, next to my home and family, the school is the most special place in my life.

This book came through me with mixed emotions. It is the expression of a large part of me that longed to be expressed. It is not exclusively my account, but also the accounts of many whom I encountered along the way. It is filled with the good, the bad, and the ugly. In no other profession could I have lived such a wide range of experiences as I have in public school education. Nowhere else could I have observed the lives of thousands — students, teachers, and parents — and been the eyewitness to so much. In no other profession would I have seen the world from such a unique, intimate, and emotional vantage point. I have been lucky to have been a public school teacher and administrator.

In schools, there are raw emotions — from despair and joy to frustration and confusion. The enthusiasm I have seen in teachers and students and felt myself have been matched by the complacency exhibited at other times. Schools are the barometers of life and I have ridden up and down that scale many times over these last 44 years. Schools reflect life in a starkly realistic manner. They are a microcosm of the world inside a school building.

Education, formal and informal, is a human institution that interacts with the world around it like no other institution. Education does not exist alone in a vacuum; it relates to and reflects the world. Education is the world! What happens in the small world of the school also takes place in the larger world and vice versa.

Ask The Janitor aims to fit in the world as a reflection of what we are doing as people. It is based on education, but is rooted in life. It is seen through the eyes of a person who began a fascination with school while attending kindergarten and has never lost that fascination in spite of many discouraging moments.

Fortunately, I had wonderful teachers growing up in the public school system of the small, but densely populated city of Hoboken, New Jersey, across the Hudson River from New York City. My elementary school, known as a grammar school in those days, was widely considered to be on par with any private school due to the academic excellence of its teachers and their dedication to the students. In the 1950s and 1960s, long before the formation of teachers' unions, teachers were considered to be "de-facto" parents; they were of a different stripe then.

If my teaching career had proceeded as smoothly as my schoolboy school career, this book would never have developed. After four years away at college, I returned to my public elementary school as a sixth grade teacher. There, I quickly observed the changes that had taken place in the building. No longer was my alma mater considered on par with a private school and no longer was there a fully dedicated faculty. The intervening years had brought with them not only a new type of teacher, but also a new climate to the school. The student body was now largely Latino and the climate ghetto-like. Silk stocking it was no more nor would it ever be again. A Federal program had been instituted that encouraged cities and towns to invite low-income students from Puerto Rico in exchange for millions of dollars in Federal funds.

I taught five years at that school and saw everything from a corrupt, dishonest administration to chaotic classes and careless teachers. Students were looked upon as pigs by some teachers and many others were there to collect their salaries and nothing more. After all, how could anyone teach a pig?

In one incident, the proceeds of a successful $12,000 candy sale were nowhere to be found only a year later. The building administrator had promised to take care of everything regarding the candy sale including depositing the money in the bank. He told everyone that he had banked the money, but neglected to mention that he had banked it in his own account.

This was the kind of administrative dishonesty that I observed as a 22-year old first-year teacher. How disheartening! There were, of course, some caring teachers, but many others who could care less. There were teachers dedicated to their students mixed in with teachers dedicated to themselves. It was a politically charged school system, so those who were politically connected could do whatever they wanted without fear of consequences.

The Vietnam War was raging and the fabric of society was being torn apart. The hours of employment allowed teachers to hold a second job that sometimes earned them more money than teaching. The popular after-school job back in those days was selling real estate. It was easy for teachers to sell real estate since their teaching hours were over by 3pm, just in time to meet clients.

After those first five years in an urban setting, I began a 27-year career as teacher/supervisor/administrator in a northeast New Jersey public school system. A rural school district when I began, it had developed into a quasi-urban one by the time I left. Second generation European students moved out making room for Asian and Latino immigrants. During the time I taught there, about 3,000 students passed through my classroom door. Countless teachers, some good and some not so good, crossed my path over the years giving me a unique perspective on what goes on inside a public school.

I quickly learned that the one thing one can always count on in public school districts is politics. It was, and still is, standard operating procedure that every important decision, and some not-so-important ones too, was made through the eyes of political connections. In the public school system, politics is the rule of thumb. Nothing is made, created, invented, purchased, or thought of without considering the political ramifications.

It was incredible for me, a naïve and idealistic young man, to realize that even teaching schedules were customized and fashioned by politics. "Politics" means that City Hall, and not the Board of Education, makes decisions concerning the operation of the schools. Politics does not just influence public school education, politics *is* public school education. It is as simple as that. Whenever there are politics in a school, you find ineffective education and teachers who are given permission not to care by political bosses — their "rabbis" in the district. By rabbi, I mean a politician who appoints people and looks after them in a protective manner with the expectation of votes in return.

This book was conceived out of the utter despair and frustration I experienced when faced with these politically charged scenes. Year after year, my intolerance over ineffective schooling did not allow me to rest and join the crowd. I refused to give in to what was the conformity of the prevailing negativism of the day. In teaching children, we were dealing with the future and the future must never be forsaken both for the sake of the children and for our own sake. Hence, the labor and birth of this writing took place with the sincere understanding that it had to help not only the individuals in our public school system, but our society at large. Improving the public school system will, in turn, improve all of our lives.

We live in a wounded world. Over the last five decades we have fought wars that have made us angry and tripped through a world of drugs. We have suffered from broken families as a result of nearly 65% of all marriages ending in divorce, some very quickly. We live in a society that has no real heroes, and to fill that void, we readily accept artificial ones whether on the playing field, the entertainment industry, Congress, or The White House. Our distrust of elected officials is widespread and, as chronicled in many opinion polls, we have little respect for our senators, congressmen, and local officials.

We have elected weak politicians, elected officials who are more interested in being re-elected to a life-time job than they are in doing right by their constituents. Many of these weak politicians use their positions as stepping stones to campaign for higher office. The greatest threat to American society seems to be coming not from foreign despots, but from within — in America, the enemy lies within!

Although we see their feet are made of clay, we continue to worship sorry excuses for heroes and, in some cases, elevate them to superstardom. Crowds of paying fans cheered a baseball player who spit in the face of an umpire. Thousands gave a hero's welcome to an NBA basketball player two days after he was arrested for raping two sisters, 13 and 14 years old. Legions applauded a heavyweight boxing champion when he was arrested for beating up his wife. Fans cheered a multi-million dollar basketball player when he criminally assaulted his coach for riding him too hard during practice. The NFL commissioner downplayed the assault of a popular player who beat up his wife in an elevator by saying that he had not seen the video. Equally unbelievable, Americans gave 79% approval rating to a President after he had a string of sexual affairs and then lied about them when confronted in a legal deposition. In contemporary American, bad boys are good and good boys are absent.

These symptoms are suggestive of a diseased society and indicate just how distorted our ethics and morals have become. We live in a violent, drug-oriented environment where the sense of law and order is skewed. Guns are everywhere. One can easily lose count of the crimes involving guns. When we value the misdeeds of violent felons and applaud their behavior, it speaks to the advanced stage of societal decay from which we suffer.

Violence can strike anytime. While writing this book, an incident occurred at a local public high school only five blocks from my home. A social studies teacher was leaving school for the day when a man came up and shot him dead near the front steps of the school. The assailant then ran a block from the crime scene and turned the gun on himself to complete this most unusual murder-suicide. In what turned out to be a case of mistaken identity, the man believed the teacher was having an affair with his wife. To add to the heinousness of the act, both deaths were witnessed by dozens of students.

Before a cure can take place, we, as a society, must recognize and understand that violence is now present in every aspect of our lives. We must be wide awake to what is happening, because it is our society that creates the schools as they are. What we have in front of us is what we have created over the last 40 years, and to think that it can never happen where you are is foolish and myopic. Our present is the result of our past and, therefore, we cannot blame the current situation on anyone but ourselves, if it is blame we seek. A better option is to seek solutions, and that is precisely the spirit in which I offer this writing.

The book's message is for us to simplify our thinking, work from the heart, and act with common sense as a guide. Within all the chaos and violence we find in our schools today, there is also the peace we all crave waiting to be found. In the face of what appears to be insurmountable societal and educational obstacles, we can turn within to find the answers. When we begin to look within, answers emerge, subtly and slowly, but they emerge. When we begin to look at one another in a simple, honest, straightforward manner, as advocates instead of adversaries, miracles take place. It is in becoming selfless that we see what needs to be accomplished.

ACKNOWLEDGMENTS

Rosemarie Bello-Hornak, Ciara Calabrese, Nicholas F. Calabrese, Olga Diaz Calabrese, Rafael Córdova, Dr. Joseph Del Giodice, Gianluca DiMuccio, Steve Dunlop, John D. Goldsmith, Esq., Susan Kronberg, Dr. Harry Laub, Fr. Edwin D. Leahy, O.S.B., Shawn Rux, Mark Scardigno, Inna Sobel, and Antoinette Willard

INTRODUCTION

Schools are so important to the health of our nation that the very fabric of our country is affected when they become low in quality. We need to be able to count on schools to educate the future of America. If that crucial function is not done well, we all suffer as a people.

In October 2014, the e-bola virus arrived in the United States neatly packed within the body of an airline passenger after a 15-hour flight from Western Africa's Liberia where e-bola was present in epidemic proportions. The carrier arrived in Dallas feeling ill and checked into a hospital. Initially misdiagnosed as having the flu, he was sent home. A day later and still ill, he returned to the hospital and was correctly diagnosed as suffering from e-bola.

Between his arrival in the United States and the e-bola diagnosis, this man was in contact with people in a variety of places between the Dallas airport, his home, and the hospital. The medical experts posed the obvious question: "How many people has this man exposed to the virus?" Medical authorities quickly followed the proper protocols in order to contain a possible spread of the dreaded disease and prevent an epidemic.

On the educational front, there has been an epidemic raging out of control in this country for over 40 years with little or nothing being done to effectively control it. The epidemic is that of our failing schools which have, in turn, failed countless students and their families while politicians look on and pay lip-service to the problem.

Why and how has this educational epidemic taken place? Why have we allowed it to happen? And, why haven't the countless dollars thrown into the school system been adequate to stop the conflagration?

This public education epidemic has given rise to the increase in private school attendance and the advent and rise of the Charter School. Parents are frustrated by federal, state, and local officials, all of whom promise academically sound and safe schools, but have not yet been able to deliver on their promises. This situation has now affected multiple generations of school children.

The educational epidemic has been quiet and slow in developing, whereas the e-bola virus is on fire and stoked by the media. The long lasting effects brought about by the destruction of our public schools, particularly inner city schools, could be as devastating and tragic as any caused by a virulent virus. The future has already been stolen from thousands of children, and there is little hope that the government with its empty promises will ever do an adequate job in healing this situation.

There are many strategies that can be implemented in order to create a positive school experience for our students and teachers. First and foremost, we must rid schools of political interference that only serves to corrupt the quality of education. As parents, we must refuse to allow politicians to decide who will teach and administer the schools we pay taxes to operate. Politically biased decisions have never been successful in fomenting a quality environment in our schools.

We must insist on excellence. Teachers must be hired based on their ability and their dedication to their craft and to educating the children in their charge. Teachers who are hired must actually love children and the craft of teaching. They must be educated in their discipline, of course, but it is also crucial that they teach from their hearts. As it stands now, most teachers are politically appointed and this compromises the integrity and quality of their performance.

Saying no to politicians may seem impossible, but it is only impossible if we allow it to be. Politicians work for us — taxpayers own the schools. We must get that right and make certain that politicians get it right too. We have to express it loudly and clearly. We should go to Board of Education meetings and speak out, and to City Hall, and write letters to newspapers stating what we expect. Remember that between the hours of 8am and 3pm our children are in the hands of teachers. As citizens, we have been complacent for too long. Now, as schools near the brink of disaster, we must demonstrate for excellence in the schools our children attend.

At the beginning of the last century, public school education was believed to be the great equalizer; now it is the great discriminator. Depending on your zip code, you will be in or out of a respectable school district.

In October 2014, an estimated 12,000 parents, teachers, and students assembled in lower Manhattan's Foley Square to protest the failing New York City public schools. Wearing bright red t-shirts bearing the slogan "Don't Steal Possible," these determined people had had all they could take of the unfulfilled promises made by politicians and school administrators regarding the poor state of the schools the children were attending. The slogan on their t-shirts asked an incompetent New York City public school system not to steal the possibility of their children's success — to them "possible" equals the future.

Over 200 of the 1,000 plus public schools in New York City have student failure rates of 90% in math and English. It is believed that 143,000 of the 1.1 million students in NYC are trapped in failing schools that politicians continuously promise to fix. Parents leading this crusade strongly felt that it was the school system that was failing, not their children — they were finally speaking out and speaking out loudly.

It is eye-opening to ask a politician where his or her children attend school. The answer is invariably either a charter school or a private school. When asked why they don't attend public schools, the standard answer is that they don't want their children to receive favored treatment on account of their political positions, but the truth is that they don't want their kids attending failing, unsafe, dangerous schools. The same schools, of course, become completely acceptable for other people's children.

A large part of the Foley Square demonstration was protesting the fact that New York City's mayor, Bill de Blasio, has been making political moves to prevent the formation of more Charter Schools. According to demonstrators, Mayor de Blasio has a track record of squashing new Charter Schools and parents are frustrated by the perpetually inferior quality of the city's public schools, not to mention the unsafe and dangerous environment they represent for the children. Charter Schools, on the other hand, are an attractive and effective answer for these families.

Urban schools are in trouble throughout the country. What were once majestic buildings housing several thousand students are now virtually empty, decaying ruins from which students flee in droves at full speed. What has happened to these once great buildings and where have all the students gone? All indices are down in urban schools. Whereas statistics tell only part of the story, the real story is in the anguish urban people experience. The degree of violence, drugs, and broken homes is dramatically higher. The larger the district, the larger the problems. A large inner city school district usually means a large number of minority children, and a large number of minority students usually means a large number of children living in poverty. These problems are amplified by the most obvious lack of political fairness. Inner-city schools are political houses of power with a feudal system that leaves children attending schools that are inadequate in all ways: equipment, resources, enthusiasm, and hope.

As an example, in the Summer of 2015 a "grade" scandal was uncovered in the New York City Public School System. A front page story in the *New York Post*[1], supported by an editorial in the same edition, confirmed that students' grades had been changed to make schools and their teachers look good. The newspaper story went on to say that due to the corruption, the high school diplomas in the city were worthless. The editorial also called for the Mayor to fire the Schools Chancellor.

In round numbers, New York City's school buildings number 1,000 and enroll 1.1 million students from a variety of ethnic backgrounds. This diversity is representative of many urban school systems throughout the country in places like Chicago, Los Angeles, Atlanta, and Newark, New Jersey.

A recent article in the *WSJ*[2] described the plight of the once mighty Boys and Girls High School in Brooklyn. For three years in a row, Boys and Girls received an "F" on their school report card. Overcrowded six years ago with an enrollment of 3,681 students, they now house 809. Sadly, these stats are typical for many of the largest New York City public high schools as well as for many other large urban public schools at a national level. The days when the likes of Norman Mailer, Issac Asimov, and Lena Horne attended Boys and Girls High School are long gone. Now, the few students left are mostly poor and black or Hispanic — 22% of them have special needs.

New York City currently has 178 schools that have been identified as "priority" for intensive intervention — this is approximately 20% of its schools. New York City is used here as an example or simple model for the deterioration of academics and facilities, but the problem is nationwide in scope.

In an attempt to improve the quality of public school education, the Common Core standards were created. The Partnership for the Assessment of Readiness for college and Careers, known as PARCC, created the Common Core tests and, with it, much disturbance among students, parents, and teachers in this country. In fact, it is difficult to think of anything in modern educational reform that has caused as much of a stir. What was meant as a means to assure a student's readiness for college and/or the workplace, has become a stumbling block for public school education with valuable amounts of time, energy, and money wasted. Something meant to bring people together ended up tearing them apart over arguments, opinions, and the search for answers.

Families for Excellent Schools is a New York City organization and a leading supporter of charter schools. Their CEO, Jeremiah Kittredge, has challenged New York City's mayor by demanding that de Blasio institute reforms that force "staff to reapply for these positions" at the affected schools. If carried out, this would be equal to removing tenure from these teachers. The president of the United Federation of Teachers (UFT) countered Mr. Kittredge's comment by saying that struggling schools just need more money to solve their issues.

The only two areas where people perceive public school education as superior to that of private schools are in teaching children to live in a diverse society and in meeting the needs of special education students. Americans know public schools are failing, but have not found a satisfactory way of solving this problem after investigating vouchers, charter schools, private schools, and any reform movement that has presented itself.

In a January 1998 article[3], *New York Post* columnist, Ray Kerrison, called public school education a "national disgrace." Mr. Kerrison was correct in having the courage to make such a bold statement. Where else have so many hundreds of billions of dollars been pumped into an institution with such little return of profit? If this were a legitimate business, public school education would have long ago gone bankrupt. Sadly, it has been bankrupt educationally, morally, and intellectually for years. Mr. Kerrison's words of almost 20 years ago are still true today.

SECTION I

PUBLIC SCHOOLS AND INCOMPETENCE: AMERICA'S NUMBER ONE CHALLENGE

CHAPTER 1
TEACHERS

Around the world, teachers have always been held in high esteem and teaching as a profession has been considered one of the highest callings. Generally, you didn't put the words incompetence and public schools in the same sentence, but there are very good reasons to do so now. Normally, one would not want to think of a school as a place of incompetence. The image schools ought to have is that of a place where incompetence is eradicated and turned into competence, but this image is proving to be an illusion. Schools are filled with incompetence of the most dramatic order, and this incompetence begins with teachers. Not all teachers, of course, but enough to give birth to this chapter.

In the world of public school education, the words of Pogo can set the scene, "We have met the enemy and it is us!" Students, teachers, and parents are crying out for help and suggestions to improve the educational climate. As far back as 1997, *Public Agenda* found in their study entitled *Getting By: What American Teenagers Really Think About Their Schools*[4] that public school students yearned for order, structure, and moral authority for their schools and teachers. The study's executive director concluded the report by saying, "By asking for less, we get less"[5].

The ones asking for less are the teachers. Youngsters want to be intellectually challenged, but the study also found, rather disappointedly, that public education teachers feel "under-appreciated, worked-over and defensive."[6] This attitude results in a viewpoint of their job that is "shaky about their mission and tentative about the importance of education itself."[7] Quite understandably, the study concluded by saying it was no surprise that "teachers communicate these attitudes to their students."[8] Can you imagine such a negative climate within the halls of a school building?

In a more recent study of students' attitudes towards their teachers, 50% said their teachers didn't measure up to what they expected.[9] The survey questioned 400,000 students in grades 6 to 12 in 569 schools nationwide. Students' perception of teachers is that teachers are positive role models only 65% of the time. These figures come from a periodical supported by teachers.

A certain number of teachers simply do not like their jobs. They stay in them out of convenience; the hours of employment, the security that tenure provides, and the possibility of early retirement. Yes, the job is convenient, particularly in the case of a parent who is supplementing the family income with a teacher's salary. "Why leave a convenient job?" is the prevailing attitude. As a result, some people will spend 20 to 30 years in an unhappy setting, giving a half-hearted effort, thinking that there is nothing wrong with that.

In one particular school, there were teachers who considered themselves great teachers, that is, each one thought of him or herself as great, they certainly didn't think that of one another. To ever question their merits was to take the air from their lungs. How dare anyone ask them not to drink coffee and eat cake while teaching? What nerve to wonder why they had left their class unattended while they slowly walked down to the teachers' room for a telephone call or a smoke! What audacity to ask for lesson plans on time and expect attendance at monthly department meetings! These teachers lived in worlds of which they were the center. They were legends in their own minds, but in reality they represent everything for which public school education is criticized.

The missing ingredient from American public school education is love; love of self, love of the profession, and, most lacking, love of the students. Something happened over the last 40 years on a societal level that caused this void to occur. During that time, the public school teaching profession became union-oriented taking the emphasis off the students.

The influx of foreign speaking students from Latin America and Asia also added an element of difficulty to teaching, since they arrived with extreme deficiencies in English and other subjects. But, we are speaking about the school system that managed to teach tens of millions of European students with great success during the early 1900s. The task was not looked upon as an impossible challenge, but as a job to be done. Today, for a great part of the teaching population, these are aspects that make the job too difficult, and to their minds... simply impossible. Therefore, there is an attitude of "we will run out our days with as little effort as possible until retirement."

The profile of the modern teacher is varied in gender, color, ethnic/religious background, *and* motivation for entering the field. Currently, a large number of teachers are lured by the protection of tenure and its guaranteed position for life. Many like the 8am to 3pm hours with summers off and an increasing number of women are using teaching as a source of income between the birth of their children or as a second income to pay bills.

Increased unionization has colored teaching blue and turned what used to be a noble profession into a blue-collar union protected job. Is teaching even a profession nowadays or just a convenient way to pay bills? Although many men and women are in it for the right reasons, teaching attracts and retains many who use it to fulfill their own needs and are union protected in doing so. This motivation makes for individuals interested in themselves and not in teaching our children. Only a self-centered and self-motivated person will refuse to do anything beyond the contract, even if it benefits students. To this kind of teacher, education and children are second to everything else!

In contrast to what the general public feels about public school education, teachers surveyed give high ratings to local public schools. In *Public Agenda's* 1996 study entitled *Given The Circumstances: Teachers Talk About Public Education Today,* teachers dismiss the public's criticism of schools by saying, "given societal pressures and a lack of parental involvement, the schools are doing as well as possible."[10] Furthermore, over three-fourths of teachers feel their schools outperform private schools. An amazing 86% of them are of the opinion that schools in their own communities do an excellent job, a view shared by only 55% of the public.

It was the feeling of the editors of *Public Agenda's* survey that teachers were trying to defend a beleaguered institution. Teachers cite, "failing families, declining communities, inadequate resources, fractured school boards, and top-heavy bureaucracies" that soak up their resources as "the real causes of the problems schools face."[11] One teacher in a focus group of *Given The Circumstances* said that the school system "isn't broken, society is broken".[12] That may be the case, but the question remains as to whether schools have adequately and emotionally responded to a broken society, or has the school system decided to continue business as usual and remain under the protection of the tenure laws?

But that was in 1996. What do teachers think about their jobs now? *US News and World Report*[13] had a feature story that reported teachers are not engaged in their jobs. They found that 7 out of 10 teachers are not emotionally connected to their work or are dissatisfied with their workplaces. Why is this? Mostly because teachers don't feel as though their opinions count and this prevents them from fully engaging at work. This April 2014 article was part of the *State of America's Schools* release.

A MetLife Foundation survey in 2012 found that teachers' job satisfaction plummeted 15 points from 59% in 2009 to 44% in 2011. Budget cuts, lay-offs, and job insecurity were the reasons cited. Can these numbers ever be turned around? Parents blame schools and teachers, while teachers blame "troubled families, distracted parents, and indifference to learning at home."[14] Eighty percent of teachers polled said that "parents do a worse job today than when they were in school" while only 55% of the public agrees.[15] We have two major groups in this discussion pointing fingers at each other. As recently as 2007, adults gave their schools only a mediocre "C" grade.[16]

Teachers are experiencing all sorts of unrest and discontent in their jobs. Most of it due to budget cuts, feeling as though they have to "teach to a standardized test," and watching their colleagues get laid off, according to a *StateImpact* survey.[17]

The same *StateImpact* report showed teachers' job satisfaction plummeted in the three years preceding the 2012 survey. From teachers being "very satisfied" with their jobs, the numbers dropped 15 points (from 59% in 2009 to 44% in 2011); the largest decline in the surveys' 28-year history.

The fact that many teachers are unhappy shouldn't come as a shock. Randi Weingarten, the president of the American Federation of Teachers, has said that budget cuts and the demonization of teachers or so-called "teacher bashing" by politicians has caused the growing dissatisfaction. Ms. Weingarten is critical of politicians who demonize teachers and use that demonization as their rationale for cutting budgets — teachers as scapegoats.[18]

Teachers list priorities as money, class size, and order while the public prioritizes safety, order, and the basics. Thus, order in schools is the only area of agreement. Everyone sees a lack of order as the single major cause for disruption in classrooms across the nation and agree that something must be done to make our public schools manageable. Parents and teachers also agree that schools must teach the fundamentals, reading, writing, math, and computer science, in order to establish a strong foundation in students. But when it comes to methods, disagreements quickly surface and escalate. There is no sense of humor among participants, so a battle rages on among otherwise very nice people who have turned themselves into combatants over the issue of education and its methods. Battle uniforms are worn and positions are taken. As usual, with a war-like mentality, once the lines have been drawn, there is little chance for combatants to reconsider their illogical positions. Ego comes into play and adds to this fruitless battle a dimension of absurdity.

Americans are convinced that teaching the basics is the most important goal for public school education, but most don't have confidence that public schools can do so, and, furthermore, many consider a high school diploma worthless. Even teachers doubt whether the institution they represent can do the job. It is the failure of the public school system to teach the basics that makes the public so frustrated and eager for reform, since many believe that without the basics nothing else can be taught.

Many states have incorporated standards into their public school curricula in hopes that it will guarantee a granted diploma as a true indication of a level of scholarship and not merely the result of social promotion. Americans clearly want standards in their public schools. It is the general belief that most students will thrive under such a system. There is a notion that students will do only as much as you ask them, and standards will ask them to do more than they were expected to do before.

Standards are clearly intended to place academic expectations on students and to be uniform across the board. Currently, though, most people agree that public school students don't have enough academic pressure placed upon them. Standards, of course, are to be followed by standardized tests administered by the State in order to measure the level of the standards learned.

If you can know a society by its educational goals, then our society is not aiming very high. In fact, a study showed that personal character and social skills "are more important components of career success than academic achievement."[19] There seems to be a suspicion of highly educated people as being out of touch with reality and cannot be trusted; an illuminating picture of our twenty-first century American society.

The failure of public school education in today's America cannot be over emphasized. Magazine articles, books, and experts echo these sentiments. Many of our schools are filled with corruption, nepotism, failure, inefficiency, and negativism to the point where this has been accepted by the public as incurable. This is not to say that some schools are not achieving wonderful results, but that is not, unfortunately, the case in many districts.

Our citadels of learning have been over-whelmed by the scandal-ridden schools around them. It is in urban education that this disparity exists at its most dramatic. In many urban school systems, any flicker of light is surrounded by an abyss of darkness, and since one out of every four students is attending school in an urban area, the number is incredibly high.

In their 1998 annual report, *Education Week*[20] ranked the nation's schools at a "C" average in the areas of "academic standards and assessments, quality of teaching, school environment, and the equity, adequacy, and allocation of their education resources." That was the second year in a row America's public schools received a "C" from this prestigious national publication. As late as 2007, schools had continuously received "C" grades in overall performance.[21]

Public school education began failing its clients near the mid-1960's during the Vietnam War, and it continues to fail in educational, emotional, and other significant ways. More than any other public institution in this country, schools have become political houses of power where children are mere pawns.

Public schools provide politicians with the means to reward or punish their followers through granting or denying jobs and promotions. It is common for positions and promotions to happen in direct proportion to potential vote getting power and not the educational preparation or ability of the person. Schools routinely place price tags on principalships and other administrative positions, so qualified people with sterling degrees must either play the game or remain stalled in their careers. In some cases, playing the game means small bills in an envelope with no questions asked. If this happened in only one school in the country it would be too many. The fact that it happens way too often makes it a national disgrace and a shame for us all.

We allow politics to play games with our children's future every time we allow an appointment or promotion to be based on political greed rather than on qualifications. What irony that the very institution designed to educate our children does not respect an academically accomplished person unless he or she is willing to play under a political tyranny. We blindly look the other way as misfit, unqualified, maladjusted, uncultured, emotionally disturbed, sexually perverse and, believe it or not, near illiterate individuals are escorted into the ranks of the faculty in our public school system all because they know someone of political importance. In many school systems, a day beyond three years of employment, these oddballs are granted tenure and protected to enjoy a 30+ year free ride doing as little as they can and making as much as possible at the taxpayers' expense.

Have you ever noticed how many public officials send their children to charter or private schools using the excuse that they do not want their political office to affect their children if they were in public schools? Some also use the excuse of wanting a religious eduction for their children. This, of course, is nonsense and politicians know it. They don't want their children to attend public schools because of the inferior level of education they would receive there.

Politicians are applauded for spending more and more money on our schools, but we don't seem to realize that in spite of all the money spent our schools have gotten worse. Money is not the answer. What we need is to understand and agree on what is wrong with the system. Once we understand, we can go on to demand more of our tax dollars from our teachers and administrators.

Foundational problems must be given priority over irrelevant minutiae. Tenure for teachers and administrators, for example, must be replaced with either periodic testing or a recertification program through course work in order to match the development of new materials, technology, and teaching methods. Many teachers are still using materials and methods they learned in college 30 years ago, way before the idea of having computers in the classroom was ever conceived. In fact, some teachers have been using the same dittos, mid-term, and final exams for so many years that the paper is now yellow. These teachers, and there are many of them, have no shame or fear of consequences because tenure protects them in their insane attempt to hold on to their outmoded resources. How effective can these teachers and their materials be?

Teachers' unions are the biggest villains in this frightening scenario. Using the guise of protecting their membership from the whims of political winds, they control the very evil they proclaim to prevent by financially supporting huge lobbies in State capitals and in Washington D.C. to insure their main item is untouched, and that main item is tenure for life. Take away this dinosaur and both teachers and administrators would march to the beat of a different drummer — that of educational accountability. Any qualified, hard-working public school educator would welcome this effort to rid public schools of incompetent teachers. It is only the insecure and ill prepared who cry foul in the battle for reform. To these loafers, lifetime tenure is the golden safe-guard for lifetime comfort. To the qualified and hard-working, lifetime tenure means little. These well-deserving people would do an outstanding job under any circumstances.

Professor Rosetta Marantz Cohen from Smith College in Massachusetts has examined the low status of teachers on a global basis. This is not a challenge just here in the United States, but a deep worldwide concern. Professor Cohen realizes that in a career, one teacher works with almost 5,000 students and underlines how important teachers are to the society. She goes on to say that good teachers and good teaching are a "cost-effective way to resolve the deepest, most entrenched problems in our society."[22]

Education Week reported an unbelievable story: "Most fourth graders who live in US cities can't read and understand a simple children's book, and most eighth graders can't use arithmetic to solve a practical problem."[23] They go on to say that "performance is worst in high-poverty urban schools, where the majority of students are poor. In these schools, two-thirds or more of students perform below the basic level on national tests."[24] A friend who owned a McDonald's restaurant told me that 17 year-old high school applicants often misspelled the name of the city in which they lived when completing an application for a position. Furthermore, *Education Week* reported: "Urban districts such as Chicago, Denver, Detroit, Houston, New York and San Francisco report that test scores are rising. But the achievement gap between urban and non-urban students in most states remains high, as does the gap between minority and non-minority students within cities."[25]

In 2010, *Public Agenda* polled a nationwide survey and found that only 52% say that math and science are adequate. Moreover, 70% of parents want more money spent on science education.[26] Things have not changed in this area since the late 1990s. The state of the country's urban schools is dismal and has the government pointing to school systems, who point to parents, who point to teachers, who point to students, who point to... The beat goes on with absolutely no change at all on the horizon.

A trend that has shown some measure of success is to have school districts taken over by the State in an attempt to improve matters. Known as "reconstitution," this method allows the worst schools to be rebuilt from the bottom up. Some reconstituted schools require teachers to reapply for their jobs. In other situations, the elected board of education and the superintendent are replaced by a state appointed board and chief administrator to run the school while the takeover is underway. In many states, consistent failure is not tolerated. These takeovers have already proven positive in the financial affairs of desperate school districts although there is not enough evidence to celebrate in the area of instruction as of yet. Reconstitution seems to be the immediate answer to schools that have proven themselves unable to help their students achieve respectable scores in reading, writing, and math.

School buildings are a testament to a different era. Not only have many city school buildings crumbled, but so have the hopes that met millions of immigrant children as they anxiously entered these schools a hundred years ago. Before their school experience was over, they had learned English and had become Americans in the process. Today, students refuse to salute the flag, come from seriously troubled backgrounds, are heavily into drugs, sex, and violence, use physical force as the one and only means to settle a dispute, and don't even know how to spell the name of the city in which they live. Every school, even those in middle or upper-class neighborhoods, finds it necessary to establish conflict resolution panels due to the pronounced level of hostility. Teachers, once pillars of the society and dedicated work-horses, are now contracted laborers with blue-collar mentalities who go by the contract and will do no more than what is necessary. Dedication is looked upon as an affront to the union. In wanting to get more, teachers find themselves with considerably less.

Nowadays, one is not guaranteed to find a public school where the climate among teachers and students is positive. Fraught with personal problems of their own, some teachers find it difficult to deal with those of their students. An increasingly large number of teachers take the "it's not my job" approach making children completely aware of this "students second" mentality.

There are schools where teachers treat students with contempt and administrators either don't care or can't care because of contractual restrictions. Why should teachers worry when politics protects them from being fired? There are administrators so afraid of teachers that you wonder what function they can possibly hold in their schools. The public school system must begin to function like a private business and treat their teachers like regular employees if it is to survive and thrive into the twenty-first century.

CHAPTER 2
ADMINISTRATORS

The school building administrator is the captain of that ship and, assisted by teachers and staff, has the job of steering the education of hundreds of children. Administration is decision making, plain and simple. Good administrators have the ability to make decisions with the welfare of those working for them firmly in mind. As a boy, I remember watching the principal of my elementary school and later of my high school doing his best to be his best. It was a time when education was ruled by talent, credentials, and merit. Sadly, nowadays, administrators are ruled by politics. The invisible hand of the politician holds the scepter to which school administrators respond.

It has become standard practice for school principals to do what they feel will win them approval from political bosses and their staffs. In striving to win this approval, they often abandon sound principles of administration so as not to risk being censured. These individuals know full well that teachers and students can create a mob scene of disfavor against them and, more often than not, this mob scene mentality would also extend to the Board of Education through the grapevine. Sooner than later, the principal in question will receive a directive from the school superintendent to cease and desist on the action taken. The superintendent gets it from the Board of Education, who in turn gets it from the grapevine, etc... Doing the right thing often metamorphoses into doing what makes the most people happy, whether it is right or not.

A school's disharmony is caused by an administrator in disharmony. For example, a principal called a meeting in which he, his vice principal, and a half dozen coordinators sat to argue over the size and shape of a conference table they were about to purchase. All the while, a few feet away, the school was rolling in mediocrity and complacency. The purchase of a table received more time and energy than the crucial issues having to do with the children's education. The latter were never even addressed at the meeting. The school was a roller coaster careening off its tracks with the principal injecting humor during the meeting to give the impression that things were under control. Nothing was under control, not even the principal himself.

A day later, I questioned a group of students as to what they thought the best method for selecting school furniture, such as a conference table, would be. Without hesitation, one of them said he would ask other administrators what tables they were using. At that, the other teens chimed in saying, "That's right, find out what other schools in similar circumstances are using." This was an easy solution to a simple problem in the minds of these teenagers. Why spend hours making such a decision?

We are in the midst of a national debate on public school education. We are in the midst of a public school revolution. From California to New York and from Wisconsin to Mississippi, Americans are dissatisfied with the system. The one thing on which everyone agrees is that change is necessary. Educational interest groups have studied what the public demands of their public schools. Safety, order, and the basics continually come up as goals, but the public does not hold much confidence in what public schools are doing to reach these goals. The feeling is that too much energy and money is being spent on an institution that has proven itself unworthy of trust as judged by the product.

Much of this malcontent comes at a time when the majority of public school students come from low-income families. Lyndsey Layton, a staff writer for *The Washington Post* wrote a feature entitled *Majority of U.S. Public School Students Are In Poverty*. I spoke with Ms. Layton a few days after the article appeared in January 2015. "With these children who are considered low-income come a host of challenges for them, for the teachers who teach them, and for the school that houses them."[27]

In her article, Ms. Layton makes reference to a teacher from an elementary school in Albuquerque, New Mexico. Because of the students in her class, this teacher begins each morning by doing an inventory of her students' immediate needs: did they eat dinner the night before, did they have breakfast in the morning, did they clean themselves, did they brush their teeth, did they sleep in a peaceful home, and do they feel safe. The answers to these questions inform her of the serious nature of these children's lives. This caring teacher has to be "counselor, therapist, doctor, parent, and attorney" for these children. Unfortunately, not every student has such a dedicated teacher.

There continues to be a noticeable disintegration of support for public school education. People continue to use private schools as a rule by which to measure the public school system, but that comparison is invalid for three solid reasons. First, private schools are able to select their students with most private schools having an entrance examination students are required to pass. Second, private school teachers don't have tenure; if a teacher's performance is below par, he or she may be immediately terminated. Third, private schools charge tuition and, there alone, a de facto segregation is enacted. Families who are able to pay thousands of dollars in tuition in addition to paying their taxes are usually the families who provide adequate cultural and educational opportunities at home. For example, private school families tend to have all the up-to-date technologies available for Junior to utilize after school hours.

Public Agenda's 1995 survey entitled *Assignment Incomplete*[28] found that 57% of parents with children in public schools would send their children to private schools, religious or non-religious, if they could afford to do so. The same report found that 66% of New York City parents would do the same if they had the money for tuition. These numbers are in addition to parents who already have their children in private schools. Public school education used to be as American as apple pie, but is now under close scrutiny and for good reason.

A more recent nationwide *Public Agenda* survey done in 2010 found only 52% of parents are happy with the math and science programs in the public schools their children attend. The survey also showed that parents wanted more money spent on science labs and computers.[29] Things have not changed much in the last 25 years.

The myopia of this situation comes into consideration when you see that public school teachers, at a rate of 88%, rate their schools as good or excellent, and 75% of them find that the public schools in their community are better than private ones.[30] Something is out of focus when there is such an odd disparity in perception. Could teachers be defending public school education only to protect their jobs?

In one school, the principal was the superintendent's hope for re-establishing stability. The challenge was that the principal, through her own insecurities, was unstable herself. She trusted no one, even those whom she had every reason to trust. In trusting no one, she began to distrust her own decisions — a sure sign of all pervading failure. She was going down fast in the middle of an icy ocean. If anyone got too close to the superintendent, this principal would feel in jeopardy. She created enemies in her mind instead of proceeding to do a good job secure in her capacity to lead. Her life became about looking backwards for real and/or imagined pursuers who could undermine her. This was an exhausting, self-imposed, fruitless exercise for anyone.

The faculty, like a pack of wild animals, could smell a fast-approaching death. They became relentless in their pressing of grievances, often frivolous, sapping the principal of her precious time and energy. As a result, only infrequently was she able to walk through the school and make her presence visible. She became a prisoner of her office, her back to the door and head in the computer, typing endless memos in an effort to correct the many faults she saw in the school — memo led to memo led to memo. After a short time, the faculty stopped listening altogether with an attitude of "Here we go again. Pay no attention to the memos!" Less writing and more walking might have done a better job.

One of the many ironies plaguing this particular school came in the shape of an attendance committee the principal formed. The committee would meet regularly to shape a new attendance policy for students. One of the faculty members who volunteered was, of course, the teacher with the highest absenteeism record in the school district. After 32 years in the system, she didn't have any sick days left and owed the school board payment in lieu of sick days used. This teacher was now about to help set an attendance policy for students when the greatest student truant did not have as many days out as she did. Not only did perceptive teachers see through this charade, so too did some astute students who wondered out loud how this teacher could possibly play a part in creating an attendance policy. By the way, she was absent for most committee meetings!

Most principals appear to have a similar personality profile; they talk tough, but want to be universally loved by students, faculty, and parents. These two attributes are usually mutually exclusive in a public school setting. The moment teachers hear you talking tough, they instantly dislike you, no matter what you say. They believe they are the only ones allowed to talk tough and that's to their students, so when a principal talks tough to them, he or she is placing them in the role of students and teachers don't appreciate that. Remember, they are protected by tenure, so they can talk as tough as they like.

Once, the principal caught two teachers derelict in their hall duty assignments. Ironically, she was not trying to catch them being negligent, it just happened. In typical public school fashion, the teachers waged a grievance against her. Imagine the nerve, they were caught negligent in their duty and they grieve it against the principal. Only in the public school system would employees have the audacity to grieve the fact that they were not doing their jobs. These two teachers, cohorts, had been AWOL from their duties for months, but when they were caught, they felt insulted. There is something in the mental makeup of public school teachers that makes them feel they are supposed to be untouchable — it is called, once again, tenure!

Principals, if they are to be effective, must demand excellence. If they are liked by their faculty as a whole, good, but faculty members who are in the profession for the right reasons will respect them. Those who look upon teaching as a cushy job with great hours and summers off, will become a dwindling minority in direct proportion to the degree to which administrators demand excellence from them.

When a principal says in October that it feels like it is June, you know that you've just witnessed an administrator in trouble; always behind and forever tired and frustrated by every comment, glance, and innuendo. Interest in being popular compromises a principal's effectiveness and fosters in him or her an attitude of defensiveness in carrying out their obligations.

Luckily for coordinators, this principal did not hold many department meetings since they were such a farce that it was getting difficult to hold from laughing. Once, a meeting was overwhelmed by a strong smell of buttered popcorn coming from a microwave in the very same room. At the conclusion of the meeting, during the coordinators' input, I suggested that we show a movie at the next meeting to match the smell in the conference room. No one laughed.

Another pathetic moment happened over the "Teacher of the Month" award. In a further effort to gain the faculty's affection, the principal decided to institute a monthly award to be distributed on a seniority basis. One particular month, she gave the award to the 32-year veteran known for being absent. The principal went on the school-wide public address system and lauded the many merits of this veteran teacher. The teacher, though, never heard a word of it — she was absent that day!

One final incident took place when the superintendent handpicked the elementary school vice principal to be his executive assistant. This person was promoted mainly to give her latitude to work in a high school as the superintendent's eyes and ears in order to force the inept school principal to resign. Within six months of the appointment, the principal had taken an extended sick leave with resignation at its conclusion. The ineffective administrator would no longer be seen in the school system — the superintendent had gotten his wish. For the following six months, the superintendent's executive assistant became the school's interim principal, but come the summer the position was made permanent.

All seemed to be going according to plan, but things were boiling under the surface with the faculty. The new principal's vice principal was an energetic and extremely competent man, and by Christmas, the principal had already butted heads with a number of faculty members. She had written disciplinary letters for some of them for having left early the day before Thanksgiving and the Superintendent had also written letters for their poor attendance records over the previous five years. Egos were steaming and a battle was about to take place. The teachers who had been written up signed petitions and made a grievance against the principal alleging that she had removed the sign-out book that day making it impossible for them to sign-out.

All this ill will was going on as the school was undergoing renovations and a growing number of teachers were developing skin rashes and pulmonary difficulties as a result of the polluted environment resulting from the construction. The construction itself was a matter of politics as usual. The American Disabilities Act had threatened a costly daily fine if certain handicap accessible considerations were not made by a certain date. Of all the contracting companies available in the area, the bid was won by a company overseen by a former board member whose political party was now in power. The situation would have been absurd enough without the next scene in this comedy of horrors. In disturbing the ceiling tiles, the fiberglass, moles, and fungus in them became airborne causing the various skin rashes and respiratory problems being experienced by teachers and students alike.

The ailments ranged from temporary, minor afflictions to concerns that would or could affect the sufferers' quality of life. One teacher developed asthma and was forced to seek workman's compensation since the illness caused her to be absent for months. Beyond that, her future health was in question — her once bright future was now dim. At home, she lived on an inhaler and was emotionally despondent. Plans of continuing her teaching career and studying for an advanced degree were no longer feasible.

Throughout this, 750 children were being housed in this school seven hours a day. A number of them also developed unexplained rashes and breathing abnormalities. Oddly enough, the teachers continued attending school in spite of the seriousness of their complaints. Not only that, but the teachers' association did not present a complaint or stage a job action of any type in their defense. Even the principal took ill from vague, undefined illnesses.

The morass of money, staffing, and programs in many inner city schools is mind boggling. The bigger the school system, the bigger the confusion. Too often, as a school system grows in complexity, it shrinks in academic productivity. It is also common to observe that as the budget increases, student performance decreases. How can this be? Would this happen in business? Schools are self-perpetuating bureaucracies that defend themselves from outside forces attempting to make them more efficient and streamlined.

Change is not accepted in the educational system. It protects its corruptness and academic bankruptcy no matter what the cost in money or in student performance. The system is the very engine that stalls the train from moving forward, and this train is an expensive one for all involved: taxpayers, students, and the reputations of administrators and teachers. No one prospers under such a climate, but these climates prosper in all too many schools. This type of system feeds on itself and on anything made available to it. It is parasitic in nature.

This type of corruption is best seen in New York City where school systems are paid State monies for the number of students in attendance. No-shows and transfer students are kept on the attendance records to keep the schools from losing money they use for salaries. By inflating attendance records, a school in Brooklyn was making an extra $200,000 a year. As a result of this dishonesty, there are phantom curriculum-listed courses that are never taught. Administrators and teachers are in on this scam, but are never held accountable when caught. In fact, according to a *New York Post*[31] exclusive, several have been promoted after it was discovered they had been part of this practice.

Schools may teach democracy and its ways in the second floor social studies class, but practice a mafioso type government in the administrative wing. Scandals are widespread, but penalties are few and far between. When we turn our heads from corruption, it means that we don't care. These people are out for themselves. They lie and cheat to keep their jobs and those of their cronies. If the private sector conducted business this way, it would quickly go bankrupt and a criminal investigation would be launched. In the school system, we promote the perpetrators to higher office. We honor the dishonorable. We cook the books to make the lies appear real. Whistleblowers face chastisement and are demoted for having the nerve to do the right thing.

The effort and energy required to create this kind of scam is Herculean. Records must be doctored and that involves the work of several people. People's values are altered to do the cheating. Students are kept on the rolls at the cost of honesty and integrity. Those in charge don't believe that money is actually being stolen. They rationalize that the cheating is keeping friends and colleagues employed, and that is a good thing. The rationalization goes further when they say, "no one is hurt by what we are doing." The truth is that everyone is hurt when this sort of illegal action takes place. Money is being stolen from taxpayers to pay for the education of non-existing students. The officials' reputations and that of the school system as a whole are irrefutably destroyed. When an institution is corrupt it is usually corrupt from the top down.

In 1998, the New York City Board of Education began a practice so elementary in nature that one wonders why it took them so long to come up with it. The city announced that it expected to demote as many as 200 principals as a result of failing scores on state and national measures. After all the failure, the Board of Education had finally decided to hold someone, anyone, accountable for the downward landslide. This was the practice the city promised to undertake, but leading a few token principals to the sacrificial slaughter on the eve of their retirement is not exactly educational reform. It was just a *coup de théâtre* to show that something was being done to correct the ills of countless mistakes.

I believe that large urban public school systems are a thing of the past and should be greatly downsized into smaller systems. New York City, for example, has already begun to divide its impossible-to-administer one million student/ one thousand building system into more manageable regions.

At the top of the administrative triangle is the superintendent. When you have a political puppet as a superintendent all hope for the school system is dashed since it is the superintendent who sets the climate in a school system. All too often, the superintendent is in place because of political favors. The appointment comes as a reward for being cooperative to the political whims of hiring, firing, contracts, promotions, and treating the favored teachers to good schedules and easy duties.

During my first year of teaching, it was curious to see two veteran teachers leave the building every day at one o'clock. Their schedules ended at 1pm so they could do their food shopping early in the afternoon. These teachers were related to politically connected people in town and the superintendent was made aware that they were to be given "early out" schedules. There was no arguing with these decisions because, in these cases, either you played ball or you were thrown ingloriously off the team. These teachers, of course, received full-time salaries for part-time work.

In some cases, politically connected superintendents make no bones about their connections. They are openly seen dining with the politicians du jour and attending political rallies and testimonial dinners. The attitude is "why worry" as long as our people are in power. As a result, the school system ends up doing whatever the politicians want instead of following plans that foster sound education for our children.

School systems are so riddled with politics that you never know who might end up being your boss. For example, a teacher, with 30 to 40 days of absence each year, rose to a position of authority in the school system where he taught. Not only was he appointed to this high position, but he counted with the unanimous support of the board members. As a result, he ruled with absolute power. Those who had given him difficult evaluations when he was a classroom teacher were in for a rocky road as soon as this man became their boss. He wanted nothing more than to get even. He made their lives miserable in all possible ways, prompting a few to seek early retirement. Those who chose to stay did so in a weakened and cowered state.

This administrative boss made his political enemies suffer. Some were publicly insulted at board meetings that he attended with such regularity that the uninitiated may have thought he was a trustee himself. Ironic how a man with such an embarrassing record as a teacher could turn into a boss who never missed a meeting of the Board of Education. He was also a fixture at the high school's football games, not because he liked football, but because the team won the championships every year. He wanted to associate with success, hoping it would rub-off on him.

School politics can turn unimportant, uninspiring individuals into political powerhouses who affect the lives of countless people. These untrustworthy school trustees are such because their new found power is used for the establishment of their own personal agendas and has nothing to do with the betterment of the school system.

In another example, a disagreement over a school dance policy demonstrates how these petty despots try to control only for the sake of power. A newly appointed high school principal wanted school dances to be open only to students in the school, but the district's school board president, in a power struggle, took the opposite position by wanting the dances to be also open to their friends, even if they did not attend the school in question. The issue escalated to wartime proportions as the principal and the board president squared off for battle. They both pressed their issues by urging students to take sides on what was now becoming a red-hot topic.

Legions were summoned to appear and speak at school board meetings. The children, in turn, asked their parents to participate. Signs were made and carried at the meetings. Petitions were circulated and signatures were sought. Lines were drawn for war — war over the issue of whether outsiders should be allowed to attend a high school dance! This much energy was not expended over the latest SAT test. Families were split apart over this ridiculous non-issue. The Civil War did not see as much adversity. It may seem absurd, but this occurs all the time in the name of power; power that is wasted energy and has no positive result.

Another example that shows where some administrators place their priorities had to do with the storage of state restricted materials known as "Special Review Assessment" or SRA for short. The materials took up the space of a storage box approximately one foot wide by two feet long. This box was to be kept under lock and key, but readily available in case the state wanted to monitor the school records for any reason. Having been given the job of coordinating this SRA work for our school district, it was my responsibility to find a safe and secure cabinet or other storage location. When I inquired about a suitable place, the principal informed me that no such place existed and that we would have to look for one at our earliest convenience.

At about the same time, the principal was attempting to curry favor with the office secretaries, who loathed her, by buying them a microwave and a two-drawer file cabinet with a lock so they could store their coffee and popcorn. Yes, popcorn! Having a microwave gave the secretaries the perfect excuse to pop buttered popcorn all day long, and they did just that.

The principal felt that coffee, popcorn, a microwave, and currying favor with the secretaries was more important than keeping the state mandated, restricted materials safe. In any case, the purchase of the microwave only made the secretaries' disrespect grow. The principal's ploy to get in their good graces was read as weakness. In trying to win over the secretaries, she had lost them even more. And, on top of everything else, the SRA material went without a home.

This kind of situations are not limited to the schools, but are also found at the level of the School Board of Education. One particular trustee, an unsavory character to say the least, reeked of egomania and was eager for power. Through a series of moves, he managed to become board president. His tenure had two stages interrupted by a time when he was unseated, so his return to the board was a tremendous victory for his ego.

During his first term, he acted as though he would do all in his power to prevent my advancing, but during his second try, he wanted to be thought of as my ally. What happened to change his mind? The factor of change was the newly appointed superintendent, a highly recognized administrator well on his way to turning the school system around in the right direction. This superintendent thought very highly of me, entrusted me in a position of power from the very first day of his administration, and was proud to say that I had been the first to support him and that my loyalty was being repaid. By appearing to befriend me, the board member intended to curry favor with the superintendent.

CHAPTER 3
LIBRARIANS

A public school library is meant to be a citadel of knowledge, an inner sanctum where students and teachers are allowed to mingle with the writings of great souls. Libraries house thousands of books, magazines, computers, and CDs, allowing students to travel around the world and into distant galaxies through these various media. Libraries are sacrosanct because of the function they perform in a public school building – much like a sacred place within a temple.

Nowadays, most students and teachers have smart phones, making the ability to research easily accessible — just google and you'll have an answer. Notwithstanding, public school libraries continue to have the special aura of a place where you can find peace and quiet and the answer to questions of research and technology. Libraries are staffed with trained librarians who are there to guide and help students with their inquiries. Although libraries continue to be places of quiet, there is usually the chatter of an interesting project going on between student and librarian. In any case, this is the function that public school libraries were historically designed to accomplish.

The true experience of a public school library, however, can be very different from this idealized version. Way too many public school librarians falsely believe their names are on the deed to the library they represent and take dictatorial ownership of the place, making it known that they "own" the library and nobody can take it away from them. These misguided librarians put out an energy that says to students and teachers alike, "You are not welcomed here!"

Public school librarians who don't want their libraries used are first cousins to teachers who don't like students. These librarians consider their libraries as homes away from home and they will not have students "dirtying" it up. I once witnessed a school principal ask a librarian to have the bookshelves cleared and wall space vacated in order to have the library painted, carpeted, and fitted for new computer wiring — the librarian refused. A confrontation ensued ending up in a stand-off between principal and librarian.

Teachers immediately took sides and pupils were pitted against pupils. Faculty cafeteria arguments became heated between the "do's" and "do not's" while much more relevant school and world issues went unexamined. The librarian was ready to deny the library a new coat of paint and computer wiring just because she intensely disliked the principal. This was a personality conflict with neither side willing to give in. Finally, the stand-off was settled when the threat of insubordination was leaked to the librarian. She may have relented, but hated the principal even more as a result.

There is an art to giving the illusion of welcome in a school library when the reality is a firm "stay away." Imagine closing a school library for an hour a day at mid-day so the librarian could have lunch? Lunch hour is the ideal time for students to use the library. Imagine prohibiting the use of the library for the months of September and June so inventory can be conducted? Visualize a library that makes students feel that they can look but not touch the books between October and May? This is not a fictitious scene in some make-believe school library, it is a fact of life in our schools today. To deprive even one student of the library's valuable resources, not to mention of the sense of adventure they could achieve through exploring world literature is beyond all imagination, but it happens!

Books not returned on time are books that librarians consider stolen and punishment must be meted out in retribution. Librarians even have a profile of the type of student they want using their libraries; students who do not fit that profile are unwelcome. Their favored profile indicates students who do not walk into the library, but float in without wearing out the carpet. These students look at the books, but never check any out. In fact, these ideal students don't even occupy seats in the library and always direct questions only to the librarian so she can demonstrate her knowledge to the world. They do not want "their" libraries used, but only looked at from a safe distance. The expression "you can look but you'd better not touch" came from these librarians.

CHAPTER 4
SCHOOL SECRETARIES

For the purpose of security, many schools now require visitors to be buzzed in at the front entrance by way of an intercom system. Sometimes, there is a metal detector through which the visitor must pass, much like the ones at airports. Once inside the building, the visitor is escorted to the main office where the clerical staff greets them and asks what business brings them to the school. It is not unusual for main office clerks to greet dozens of visitors each day: parents who come to pick up children, salesmen who have appointments to meet with personnel in charge of buying supplies, and many others who come for various reasons.

The office clerks, sometimes called secretaries, are the first people representing the school when they greet visitors. One could say that the office secretary is the "face" of the school. Generally speaking, they are friendly and courteous and make visitors feel welcome.

In my experience, however, some secretaries are unbelievable in an unbelievable way! In one of the schools I taught in, for example, among the three office clerks there was not one true secretary. Appointed by politics, they were secure in knowing that they could stay there forever without any threat of accountability. Although they did not have tenure as teachers do, their "tenure" was assured by their political connections. Their positions were solid and secure for life.

One had to marvel at their complete disregard for telephone manners. Callers would inform me of the difficulty they had had in reaching me and wondered if the school had been closed for the day since no one answered their repeated calls to the main number. The secretaries were never in a hurry to answer a call, particularly if they were busy chatting on the phone themselves. Getting a telephone message in your mailbox meant that the call had come in hours before, sometimes even days!

Moreover, these secretaries would engage students in heated arguments over absences and tardiness. They acted like school principals at any opportunity they had; to say they were out of bounds was to say the least. Hurting students with their words and attitudes was their forte. If someone had done the same to their children, a war would have ensued, yet they thought nothing of doing it to other people's children.

School secretaries are more interested in being an active part of the gossip mill than in the orderly functioning of the office. They set up their own version of the Internet with their penchant for gossip. The concept of a confidential secretary is a thing of the past when it comes to school secretaries I have observed — to them there is nothing confidential anymore. Secretaries who can't type surely know how to spread stories about students, parents, teachers, administrators, or anyone else who gets in the gossip line of fire.

These secretaries were rude both on the telephone and in person, they were downright abrasive. People calling would tell me that when the telephone was answered they could hear the conclusion of a conversation the answering secretary was having with someone in the office. At times 10 or 15 seconds of this conversation would be clearly heard before the secretary would respond by saying, "High School" followed by a pause. If a caller was a first time caller, imagine the impression they would have of the school. This lack of telephone etiquette spoke volumes about their attitudes. It said, in part, "Go ahead and complain because I can't be fired no matter what I do." Sadly, they were correct!

There are millions of school secretaries throughout the country who are polite, courteous, and do the right thing, but where politics allows them to do whatever they want and feel invincible, they become another dead weight around the neck of our educational system.

SECTION II

TERRIBLE TENURE

CHAPTER 1
TENURE PROTECTS WEAK AND LAZY TEACHERS

There are countless dedicated public school teachers who go to work every day with a strong sense of purpose and selflessness written into their personal lesson plans. These teachers make a positive impact on the lives of tens of millions of children leaving an indelible mark that will accompany them throughout their lives. Extraordinary teachers touched my life during my school years and I remember them to this day with love and gratitude for helping to make me the man I am.

I remember many teachers who were wonderfully giving and made me feel welcomed and honored in their classrooms. Likewise, I trust that I too, as a teacher and vice-principal, was responsible for guiding students in the right direction. I know for a fact that the *Famous People Program* I created had a positive effect on thousands of students and hundreds of teachers. *The New York Times* was so impressed with it that they wrote a feature story.[32]

Be that as it may, one of the most questionable developments in the history of public school education has been the adoption of tenure for teachers. In many schools, after three years and a day of teaching, a teacher is guaranteed a job for life. Originally intended, from a historical perspective, to protect teachers from the vagaries of politics, it has become an impenetrable shield for deadwood among the teaching ranks. Once tenure is granted, it is virtually impossible to remove that teacher from the classroom. Most states call for removal only after charges of incompetence or moral turpitude are found. These are difficult charges for a Board of Education to substantiate in court, thus the "rubber room" in the New York City school system where unfit teachers are housed at full salary.

Tenure gives public school teachers a feeling of invincibility and an unearned sense of authority. A large percentage of them seem to think that when tenured they can do whatever they want, when they want, how they want. Their actions yell out that they cannot be touched or held accountable for anything. Tenure has become a reason to take enthusiasm and work ethic down a notch or two. Under the worst conditions, tenure kills the soul of a school by allowing lazy teachers to do a minimum amount of work for years on end. Not all teachers take such a subversive path, but those that do make this situation painfully familiar to enthusiastic teachers who must then carry the load of those who don't care much. It surely can be described as "terrible tenure" when many use it for their own profit and not for the reasons for which it was intended.

More and more, the notion of tenure sticks out as a poor public relations issue for teachers, and therefore, states are questioning its value. You would think teachers would welcome some form of periodic recertification to secure their place, but most of them and their associations are putting up a good fight to keep the tenure laws in place exactly as they are. They cite school politics as a reason to preserve tenure while in reality they just want to hold on to a good deal unhampered by authority.

Politicians are just as guilty in this matter, maybe more so. The vast majority of elected officials look to the voting power of teachers to keep them in office; disturbing this sleeping giant would be political suicide even though the climate in many schools and the education of millions of children would improve. Politicians talk tough, but act weak in terms of eliminating or even reforming the tenure laws. They are afraid to discuss the issue, after all, you are talking about people's livelihoods when tenure is being discussed.

The public needs to speak up loudly. The closest anyone has gotten to modifying tenure laws has been making teachers take college courses every few years in the name of educational improvement. There is much debate that tenure ought to be contingent upon the successful completion of these courses, but the operative word here is debate because nothing has been accomplished. No state or politician dares to deal with the tenure issue head on for fear of making enemies of the teachers' unions. Tenure no longer holds merit — let's do away with it.

In the Baltimore city schools, a recent inventory uncovered evidence of the dance of the lemons in which school bureaucrats shuffle unproductive teachers from school to school. If tenure laws were not so all protective, these people could be let go and kept away from schools so their actions and/or inactions would not affect our children. Tenure laws, as they stand, keep inefficient teachers in schools where they can inflict even more damage to a school system already plagued by enough challenges. The end of tenure would bring about the end of this kind of abuse and would set these "professionals" free so they could go and try their luck in some other line of work.

In many ways, terrible tenure has made teachers lazy and neglectful. One of the best ways to observe this is by taking a look at the way teachers dress. There is a percentage of teachers who dress not only sloppily, but almost appear to be in competition with their students in what they wear. There is an "I don't care" attitude in their dress and it has much to do with the sense of invincibility that comes with tenure. Another way to observe this complacency is in the way they speak, emulating students' speech instead of teaching proper English by example.

As far back as the 1990s, the Board of Education in the district where I taught, passed a resolution outlining a code of dress for teachers. The joke around school was that Dr. Muciaccia would have to dress down to meet these new requirements, since I always believed that teachers should dress in a professional, appropriate manner.

For years, we have placed our trust in teachers, administrators, and school boards to make decisions about managing schools. As long ago as 1994, a survey by *Public Agenda* entitled *First Things First: What Americans Expect from the Public Schools* showed a crack in the sacred vessel of public trust. A third of those surveyed said that teachers were worse then than when they were in school.[33] The outward indications are dress and language. This subtle change in perspective on the part of the public is significant and must *not* be ignored.

In a study done by the *Program on Education Policy and Governance* (PEPG) from the Harvard Kennedy School in Cambridge, MA, it was determined that the public is willing to invest more money into their schools and that they only give a "C" grade to schools.[34] We can conclude that the American public has experienced discontent with their schools for at least the last 25 years, if not more. It is no wonder that a *Public Agenda* survey from 2010 found that *only* 52% say math and science is fine as it is on a nationwide portrait.[35] That same study found that, internationally, US students rank 25th in math and 21st in science. Once the world leader, we are now dismally behind the world in our science and math abilities.

In the focus groups of this *Public Agenda* survey, the public was outspoken enough to say that they could not believe that there had been no firings in their district's public schools and that they felt the faculty should be downsized the way businesses downsize to get rid of personnel who are not profitable. There are now "large numbers of Americans (who) wonder whether too many teachers are too lax, too easy-going and too quick to let the youngsters run the show." Tenure is great in many ways, but it does protect teachers who should not be teaching. Tenure is clearly its own worst enemy in cases such as this because it flaunts ineptitude in the face of the public.

Tenure prevents public school education from showing an educational profit. It does this by making all teachers, even outstanding ones, be content with the lackluster worlds they create within their classroom walls. As a result of this posture, there is no real interest in or concern for the schools at large. Public school teaching has lost its status as a profession by becoming a unionized, blue-collar job that attracts the benefit-conscious more than the student-oriented. If we believe, as *First Things First* told us in 1994, that good teachers "are the single most important ingredient in sound education and good schools," then good teachers are fewer now than ever before.

If a private business was suffering declining sales due to outmoded policies, it would revamp its ways and show a profit, or it would go out of business. The American automobile industry was nearly put out of business by the Japanese during the 1970's and 1980's. The American monopoly on the automobile market right after World War II caused the industry and its workers to become unresponsive to the public's cry for a better car, so Japan saw an opening and responded from 10,000 miles away. That response was exactly what Americans wanted — a better automobile at an affordable price. American automobile ingenuity needed 20 years to catch up after the Japanese, German, and other foreign imports took over the market; some would say that it has never really recovered.

The public is now desperately asking the public school education industry to respond in a similar way. This accounts for the rise of charter schools that are considered to be public schools in the private interest. All signs point to the fact that public school education is failing Americans now as the automobile industry failed them then. The call for a revolution in public school education is afoot in America and at its core is an outcry for the elimination or complete modification of the tenure laws. Change at an institutional level can only occur when participants adopt different, innovative strategies in performing their duties. The public is calling for education to do so now.

Founded one hundred years ago, the Brookings Institute, based on Embassy Row in Washington, D.C., calls itself an "American centrist think tank." In their most recent report[36] they talked about "A deep divide between the opinions held by citizens and those who teach in the public schools." That divide is most profound in the areas of teacher pay, unions, charter schools, required testing, vouchers, and teacher tenure reform.

In reviewing the Brookings Institute article, former New York City school chancellor Joel Klein stated that "While teachers tend to support the status quo, the public is increasingly looking for major changes." An impressive statement from the man who once administered the largest public school system in the country!

Renewable tenure would be an objective, impartial method of determining whether teachers are qualified to continue in the classroom. Teachers should be tested every five years with an instrument similar to the National Teacher Examination (NTE) that would itself be reshaped every few years. Newer issues, skills, techniques, and technology would be included to encourage teachers to stay current. Imagine a physician who is unaware of new procedures in medicine. Would you allow yourself to be treated by one?

Tenure took the climate of cooperation away from our schools, turning them into places where teachers refuse to begin work a minute before contract or continue work a minute after. Contract agreements might have been thought of as gainful for teachers, but what they have lost in terms of working-place climate and morale is devastating to all concerned. Schools have become unrecognizable because of tenure rights. It protects weak, lazy teachers and, as a result, dedicated teachers suffer.

Public school education makes for a deceitful climate among the teaching staff thanks to the political nature of the system. The preponderance of politically based teaching appointments is so evident that there is little quality control assurance. Once appointed, these teachers gain tenure and are thereafter among the untouchables of education. They can neither be fired nor given assignments that don't meet with their acceptance because their tenure guarantees that.

As far as an uninvited assignment is concerned, politically powerful friends insulate politically connected teachers from any such assault on their egos. The tail wags the dog, much as you have in professional sports when a high-priced athlete refuses to follow the direction of a lesser paid and not so well known coach.

A naïve high school principal once asked me how the business world handled employees who refused to follow direction. I answered, "They fire them." The principal was incredulous. He had been in public school education all his life and knew that tenured teachers were virtually impregnable from being fired or from being disciplined for poor performance. Businesses are interested in the bottom line because the bottom line means money. Education is interested in feathering the nests of politicians and that means making political supporters happy.

In one high school, the idea of changing the format to block scheduling came as a shock to many on the faculty. The new format would change the schedule from the traditional six, seven, or eight periods of 40-minute classes to that of three or four classes of longer duration. These longer periods, usually 80 or 90 minutes in length, are intended to allow for a variety of more efficient teaching methodologies. Nation-wide results have been positive.

As the school approached the start of block scheduling, the negative "Teachers' Room Syndrome" came out in force. In this room, teachers privately discuss what annoys them; subjects they would never discuss at meetings with school administrators. Those who looked upon the change to block scheduling as work, did everything they could to sink the ship. They went so far as to circulate a 12-page packet that showed reasons not to incorporate block scheduling into a high school program. The packet included a *David Letterman's Top Ten Reasons for Block Scheduling* intended to demean the educational innovation. This hand out, offered as an underground piece of literature, was typed, photocopied, and distributed using school equipment and personnel.

Not a faculty member on the staff of fifty-five had the integrity to stand up at any of the numerous block scheduling discussion groups to question the practice and the process. Instead, these highly educated, tenured "professionals" chose to operate through clandestine means. They never offered an intelligent challenge to block scheduling. Instead, they gave threat and innuendo. They wanted their careers to continue smoothly without the thought of changing scheduling practices or curriculum; change was the enemy. As it turned out, block scheduling was a much needed breath of fresh air to that school. It worked in the best educational sense.

Another little discussed aspect of public school education is the number of teachers who are ill suited to be in a classroom. Public schools have their share of bigots and many of these prejudiced teachers will openly discuss the failings and demerits of a particular race or religious group. Some plainly state that a certain group cannot be taught, others, a more devious group, will show their hatred in more subtle ways by giving certain children lower grades and making their assignments nearly impossible to complete. This racist, bigoted, elitist group is also protected by the current tenure laws.

Still another group of misfit tenure protected educators is made up by the emotionally and/or socially maladjusted. These teachers, some of whom have been clinically diagnosed, continue to make their living teaching our children. Every word and gesture from these teachers holds the class on the brink of chaos, but the tenure laws are so rigidly structured that firing them is difficult and costly, if not outright impossible. Schools try their best to bury these teachers in the system, often giving them the classes with the least number of students. Every student in the school knows who these teachers are and do anything to avoid being assigned to their classes. Some of these teachers have been around for 25 or 30 years and are now ready to collect life-long pensions paid by taxpayers.

In Seattle, a 35-year old female teacher was convicted of raping a 13 year-old male student. The mother of four bore the 13 year-old's child and spent five months in jail for the crime. The sentencing judge signed a no-contact order forbidding the teacher from going near the youth, but disregarding the judge's order, the teacher was arrested a few days later while in her car with the boy at three in the morning. She then became pregnant by him for a second time.

The story showed such a low standard of morals that all major news agencies carried it as a lead story. A cry of, "How could this woman have been a public school teacher?" echoed across the country. Unfortunately, this type of fraternization between teachers and children is a reality that in many cases goes unchecked. School officials, students, and parents may suspect such goings-on, but are unwilling or unable to do anything about it. These charges are difficult to substantiate, so way too many maladjusted people get to spend time with our children on a daily basis.

One such teacher was forever at war with her small class of students — one of her classes had only four! She had been diagnosed with a psychological disorder and was prone to plunging into bouts of darkness where she would stay for days. Medication did not do much for her. She would react to real and/or perceived attacks in some of the most irrational ways possible. During one of her many public fits, she sat crying in a fetal position in the main office as teachers, secretaries, students, and parents observed her behavior. She was a pathetic case, but this pathos made her no less of a threat to a class of children. Another profession would have cast her out long ago, but public school education continued her employment and gave her yearly increments. School officials looked the other way as long as nothing serious happened even though she was a time bomb waiting to explode.

How sad for her and for the institution she represented. From the students' point of view, she was someone they tolerated. Pushed too far, some of them were ready, willing, and able to give her the fight of her life. Often, students would retreat and do no work as a result of this nonsense. They would beg not to be assigned to her class using the word "crazy" to describe her erratic behavior.

For years, this teacher ate lunch inside her car in the faculty parking lot. She isolated herself from everyone and remained in her dream world hating having to re-enter a classroom filled with students whom she could not understand, let alone teach. The various psychological and emotional profiles they brought to her attention were as foreign to her as her own. The fact that this troubled woman was allowed to teach in our public school system is decidedly one of the darker sides of tenure.

This woman's presence, and the presence of those like her, weakens every aspect of public school education. There are those who might call for tolerance of others' shortcomings and consider this criticism harsh, but in a classroom full of children there can be no tolerance of bigotry or emotional, social, or psychological maladjustment. Irrationality calls for forbearance as our classroom walls fall down around us. People going through this kind of experiences don't belong in a classroom. Classrooms demand intelligent, fair-minded, well-balanced adults to deal with the whole spectrum of problems encountered on a daily basis. To allow bigots and mentally maladjusted people to populate classrooms across this nation and then reward them with tenure and yearly increments is to underline the immediate need for reform. What maladjusted teacher would be afraid to bring their erratic behavior into the classroom when they know that under tenure there are no consequences? Change to the tenure laws will only take place when the public demands it. Public school education will certainly not censor or change itself on any account.

Education reform has become the main topic in more and more State of the State and State of the City addresses around the country. Governors and mayors are finally listening to the public outcry for more educational productivity for their tax dollars. When the teen at the local department store has a difficult time making change, there is a serious problem at hand. One governor suggested a longer school day and making school principals accountable with the possibility of losing their tenure status and their jobs, as superintendents in some states did some years ago. This way, the governor argued, principals will be responsible for the failure of their schools. Actually, the governor is falling short of proposing the necessary reforms since the removal of the whole tenure system, especially that of teachers, is what is needed.

The notion of tenure, as we know it in the twenty-first century, is obsolete. Tenure is a cloak behind which people ill-suited to be in education hide for the duration of their careers. To remove tenure for superintendents and not to propose the same for principals and teachers is incomplete. Actually, it would be more sensible to continue tenure for administrators and remove it from teachers.

Look at the situation this way: In the NBA, players are usually paid much more than their coaches. Often times, players can exert pressure on management to hire or fire a coach. But when a team is losing, it is always the coach who is axed, sometimes at a great expense to the team's treasury. The theory being that the coach didn't motivate the players enough to win. The truth is that both NBA players and public school teachers are supposed to be self-motivated professionals and should stop blaming others for their own woes and failures. If every NBA player and schoolteacher decided to become an entity to himself you would see an era of success the likes of which we have not seen in our lives.

During his time as New York City's mayor, Michael Bloomberg made his feelings regarding tenure and the city's public schools quite clear. Bloomberg opposed granting tenure to teachers. He was aware that the so-called rubber room in the city's Board of Education costs taxpayers millions of dollars a year in fully paid salaries to teachers who have proven themselves unfit to teach. Due to tenure laws, these teachers cannot be fired. From a practical, financial point of view, tenure makes no sense in the mind of a successful businessman like Michael Bloomberg. Business does not grant tenure, why should schools?

Time magazine had an illuminating cover story in October 1997 entitled *What Makes A Good School? Special Report* which informed us that 89% of all American children attended public schools. Public school educators have almost 9 out of every 10 children within their domain. The feature article also made another startling comment when it stated: "In a poor neighborhood, the public school system is often the biggest employer. Teachers, administrators and School Board members desperately want to keep their positions, even if they aren't doing a good job, and quite often there is very little pressure on them to do better."[37]

Teachers are under no pressure to improve their performance and the public seems fed up with this callous immune-to-everything type of feeling. This vested "all in the family" attitude among public schools is deficient and the time has come for accountability.

Most peculiar of all is that teachers feel insulted when asked to increase their students' basic skills. All sorts of excuses are given, both real and imaginary, for the failure of students to perform better. Teachers know that they don't have to do better to continue in their jobs and, most ridiculous of all, to receive their yearly salary increase. This flawed system of lifetime tenure takes care of a host of problems for public school teachers; it is an ideal situation for them. What it certainly does not address is the quality of our children's education and this lack of quality will in turn serve to bankrupt the future of our nation.

CHAPTER 2
"THEY CAN'T BE TAUGHT"

The idea of the self-fulfilling prophecy is too often used for the wrong reason in the classroom. Teachers claim to know the so-called "good" students from the so-called "bad" ones and treat them accordingly. Jaime Escalante, the high school teacher who inspired the film *Stand and Deliver*, liked addressing this point. He told the story of having two students named Johnny in the same class. One was well-behaved and achieved academically while the other was a class cut-up and a nuisance to teachers and to the other students. At a nighttime PTA meeting, a mother approached Mr. Escalante and introduced herself as Johnny's mother. Mr. Escalante, taking her for the good student's mother, immediately began praising the boy.

The next day, "bad" Johnny approached Mr. Escalante to tell him that no one had ever said such nice things about him, that no teacher had ever used the words "it is a pleasure to have him in my class." Mr. Escalante realized his mistake, but didn't say a word. In the ensuing days, the once "bad" Johnny became a model student of exemplary behavior who handed in all homework assignments. The child had made a remarkable turn-around thanks to his mother's mistaken identity. It is amazing to realize what a few kind words can mean in the life of a so-called problem child. The concept teachers hold of their students is all-important.

On the opposite end of the spectrum from Mr. Escalante, we have way too many teachers who take the approach of labeling students and deciding whether or not they can learn. One such teacher declared that the problems her school was confronting had been caused by a recent influx of Hispanic students. This college graduated, self-proclaimed outstanding teacher was heard saying that "Hispanics can't be taught." The school had received a large number of Hispanic students from The Bronx whose families had decided to settle in New Jersey in hopes of finding a better education for their children. They also sought to escape the daily violence experienced in their previous school districts.

Most harmful of all are teachers who dislike students. There is a phenomenon among a certain strain of teachers that involves the very real and palpable dislike they feel for their students. These teachers find many students are "un-teachable," and not liking children as a rule, they limit themselves to students who perfectly fit into a mold they have created. Anyone who doesn't fit the mold for reasons of race, religion, behavioral patterns, intellectual capacity, or personality immediately becomes un-teachable and irrelevant to them. Teachers are not alone in this, administrators can fall into this category as well. After all, principals and vice principals were once teachers and old habits die hard – if ever at all.

CHAPTER 3

RECERTIFICATION AS A POSITIVE ALTERNATIVE TO TERRIBLE TENURE

The hottest topic in education today is that of eliminating tenure for teachers. The topic is extremely personal for teachers as professionals — they believe their abilities are being called into question. It is also deeply emotional in that they feel they are fighting for and defending their livelihoods. As a result, teachers and their unions actively oppose any and all proposals for tenure law reform.

In place of teacher tenure, experts recommend a program of recertification. What is recertification? It is requiring compulsive periodical training for teachers and making the re-issuance of their license dependent upon the successful completion of the training. Recertification would take the form of courses given within the district after 3pm or courses offered through a neighboring university. The courses would be given by qualified professors in education.

When one considers that most professionals are required to keep abreast of the latest improvements in their fields by attending seminars and lectures, this proposed reconfiguration of the tenure laws is not so far-fetched. IT experts are required to attend seminars in programming and coding, and physicians and dentists could not function properly in a world of changing practices without some type of continuing education courses in their specialties.

Teachers take a different turn by holding to the notion that the outmoded strategies they learned during their undergraduate methods and materials class will suffice for the entirety of their careers. If they truly considered teaching a profession, they would readily seek out opportunities to learn more about their craft. As it stands now, teacher unions oppose recertification and find it insulting to even consider the topic. Can you imagine people whose profession it is to teach not wanting to learn? It is the closed minded effect resulting from years of being protected under tenure. A policy of recertification would be a welcomed light in this dark corner of our educational system. No professional would refuse an intelligent, judicial system of recertification using qualified college professors teaching current methods in their areas of specialty.

The question of fair teacher assessments and licensure must be raised. Given the fact that teachers are required to take education courses in college and are required to prove their ability to teach during student teaching, it seems fitting for them to be given a renewable 3 to 5 year license based on the evaluation of their building administrators and the successful completion of graduate courses in issues crucial to their disciplines.

For example, teachers might be required to take computer technology courses or specific courses relative to their teaching fields. Nutrition courses might be addressed in some cases and maybe courses dealing with the psychology of children from one-parent families since that dynamic is so prevalent in contemporary society. Drug and alcohol awareness seminars might be required coursework along with courses in STD prevention.

The possibilities of recertification courses are boundless. Not only would public school teachers be more aware of the modern world, but this emphasis would also give state and private colleges a boost in their graduate departments. Many of these courses could also be taught in public school buildings after 3pm for the convenience of teachers.

In a system where teachers are disgracefully unaware of how to work a computer or of anything to do with current events, the need for recertification becomes an unquestionable necessity. Everyone would profit from this experience. Terrible tenure protects the worst and hurts the best. Good teachers welcome recertification and the opportunities for learning that come with it. Recertification would also attract a higher quality of teacher into the system and help make teaching a profession once again.

CHAPTER 4

CONCERNS OVER THE PROFILE OF NEW TEACHERS

There are serious uncertainties about the quality of emerging teachers both from an academic and a psychological standpoint. In a 1997 *Public Agenda* study, it was reported that most education professors "have concerns about the quality of prospective teachers in their programs."[38] An amazing "7 in 10 professors of education (72%) said they often or sometimes come across students they seriously doubt have what it takes to be a teacher." In the same study, many respondents were concerned that the new entrants "lacked the passion or skills needed to be good teachers." One professor in the focus group talked about these prospective teachers not fitting the idea of a good teacher. He went on to question their academic qualifications and classroom management techniques.

Incredibly, a full 75% of the education professors in this study complained "that too many of their students have trouble writing essays free of mistakes in grammar and spelling." As a result, "67% of those surveyed endorsed, without reservation, a proposal to require teachers to pass tests demonstrating proficiency in key subjects before they are hired." One professor went so far as to state, "our profession attracts students who are at the less capable end of the academic scale."[39]

If we agree that good teachers are the most important element of a public school system, then we need to select only good teachers to teach in our schools. How do we do that? How do we define a good teacher? Surely, a focus on students must be part of a good teacher's make-up. Right?

Historically, the best minds have always gone to medicine and/or law. Education has been a distant third in requiring brainpower. Many candidates look upon it as an easy career with short hours and long vacations. The pay may be low, but that is the price you pay for the aforementioned advantages. Many teachers see the profession as an "in and out" doorway that allows for an easy exit in order to have a family and, thereafter, an easy re-entry once the children are grown and you are ready to supplement the family income. There is little need to learn the research that took place while you were out because you have tenure and there are no such requirements.

The *U.S. News and World Report* ran a feature article in their April 9, 2014 issue entitled *Most Teachers Are Not Engaged in Their Jobs, Gallup Finds.* According to the piece, among teachers "nearly 7 in 10 are not emotionally connected to or are dissatisfied with their workplaces." More than 7000 teachers took part in this particular survey. The article went on to show that among professionals, teachers were among the least likely to feel that their opinions at work counted and that their supervisors created an open and trusting environment.

SECTION III

DIVORCE AND THE CHILD

CHAPTER 1

DIVORCE AND WHAT IT MEANS TO THE SCHOOL

Scientists may speak of the twentieth century in terms of polio, AIDS, and E. Coli, but sociologists will surely define it in terms of divorce and parent's non-involvement in their children's lives. Divorce and parental non-involvement require that others raise, feed, give values to, and educate our country's youth instead of their parents. In many cases, the divorced and/or the non-involved take no responsibility when things go wrong with their children and are the first to point fingers when things get out of control. These social conditions have eaten away at the fabric of our society and destroyed the American family as we knew it. As a matter of fact, the three major culprits of the erosion experienced by our society in the last forty years have been wars, drugs, and the dissolution of the family.

These social diseases cut across all social strata. The lower class is as likely to suffer from them as the middle or upper classes. Like many diseases, divorce and parental non-involvement are not bound by money, race, or religion. They blindly leave their mark on our children no matter where they come from.

You can clearly observe these conditions in action at any after-school activity — basketball games, cake sales, PTA meetings, or Back-To-School nights. Parents are absent in droves and conspicuous by their very absence.

At a local high school of 650 students, less than 100 were represented by their parents at a typical parent's night. This dismal scene is repeated countless times throughout our nation's schools. From California to Vermont and from North Dakota to Louisiana, parents do not attend school functions to support their children's educational and social growth. Sometimes, it is lack of time in the busy life of a single parent and, sometimes, it is lack of interest.

Let us examine the motives for this no-show behavior. Everyone agrees that school is important and that our children are the most precious possessions we have; a real blessing in our lives. But, to paraphrase Emerson[40], what people are speaks louder than what they say, and what they are is absent. Just as the home is vacant when teachers turn to it for assistance in educating children, so too, is the school vacant when parents are invited to come in for a cup of coffee and a chat about their child. Parents claim that school and their children are important, but they don't act out their words. The demands placed on parents, particularly single parents, overrides participation in school activities. The stress of life is too much for parents to be more involved.

Parents who are absent when their children need them most causes another unseen problem. If parents are not involved, they are not making positive demands for school reforms. As a result, administrators and teachers can conduct business as usual like in the adage, "When the cat's away the mice will play." The "cat" is very much away in education and the "mice" have played our schools into untenable institutions where more harm is done than good.

A mother of thirteen-year old twins who sends her children to a charter school told me that she knows a teacher in her local public school who brags that she has never been formally observed by her supervisor and has never had demands made on her by her students' parents. She went on to gloat that her job is the easiest in the world — she is paid well and has little or no responsibilities. This teacher works in a public school that is in a lower level socio-economic neighborhood.

An outgrowth of divorce can be seen in psychologists' estimations that there are over three million children in this country with diagnosed depression. Children's depression can present in a variety of ways such as quietness, solitude, stealing, isolation, cutting themselves, and other abnormal activities. Most of these children come from less than nurturing home environments that are not conducive to the positive growth of a child. The baggage many kids carry as a result of an unhappy home life is enough to make anyone depressed. It is a wonder that some students function at all.

The argument of quality versus quantity is fatuous and makes no sense whatsoever. It is a device we have manufactured to make ourselves feel better in the face of an experience that has the power to demoralize us. It gets us out of the jam of negative emotions and helps us keep even-keeled. There is no substitution for being present with our spouse and children.

The high mobility in the country is also reflected in our school systems and forms part of the divorce and parental non-involvement issue. We live in an extremely mobile society. It is not unusual for public schools to have as much as a fifty percent turnover rate among students within a given school year. With this high rate of mobility, a lack of continuity occurs. Classes are disrupted and so are the lives of the children. The climate in such schools is chaotic and students suffer as a consequence. It may be that this outward mobility is also a reflection of the inner turmoil experienced by so many children as a result of the emotional coldness our society produces.

All this disruption adds to the unsettled environment in schools. It is as if drugs, violence, sex, one-parent households, and other disturbing societal elements were not enough for us to accommodate or perhaps it is because of these things that the mobility rate is so high. Nowadays, a high school senior class does not look anything like the kindergarten class of only twelve years earlier. Stability is gone and tribal ties have been broken from the days when people were united by family. It is a new, but not necessarily better day.

In terms of early education, for example, the great debate in reading textbooks is literature versus phonics, but this argument totally misses the point. The real debate ought to be about parents not being home to help their children learn how to read and how they can be convinced to be present in their children's lives. In fact, the arrow not only misses the target, it misses the tree as well. No reading program or type of textbook, whether literature-based or phonics, can replace a caring, loving parent who reads to a child.

We usually intellectualize the problem and talk about research proving one textbook more advantageous than another. We go to world renowned universities and spend great amounts of money on programs touted as "the best," when nature has already designed the greatest reading program and it is called the family. We miss the target completely when we attempt to substitute a university program for a loving parent's presence at the homework table. Nothing can replace the words, "What did you do in school today, honey?" There is no textbook, no researched program in reading, no latch-key program, no nanny, and no television show that can replace those loving words at the end of a school day. Once uttered, every child knows that the question will be a ritual at suppertime. An eagerly anticipated ritual that has "I love you" written all over it, and there is no substitution for love.

There seems to be a deep-rooted, fundamental rage that permeates the hearts, the minds, and the very souls of many of our children. This rage is the result of being raised in a society that is morphing from a two-parent, peaceful, drug-free milieu into a one-parent, violent, drug-riddled environment. This rage can even be observed in pre-K children and those in the primary grades who take Prozac, the twenty-first century answer to mother's milk. In teens, this rage engenders violent behavior.

Violence outside of and within schools has become so commonplace that it no longer demands headline status. We have become accustomed to children acting violently and instead of addressing the causes we medicate the symptoms. Discovering the "why" of the problem may get us dirty with guilt. We want things to be quiet, where "quiet" means that the problem does not exist. Examining the why shows us that our children's problems might have been prevented. Unfortunately, instead of practicing introspective examination, families are mistakenly led to believe that anti-depressants are the answer to children's problems.

Many parents choose their career over caring for their children. When this is done, we imprint an indelible mark on our offspring. These parents place their infants and children in the care of strangers in order to pursue careers that will allow them to enjoy the benefits of a higher income bracket. Mother and father go off to work and pick-up baby at 7 pm from a daycare center that even changes diapers. What a wonderfully convenient world to live in where even diapers can be changed by someone else.

Formula has replaced breast milk because the mother would have to be there to breast-feed. Changing diapers and bathing your child may get in the way of Thursday's corporate meeting. Is it so difficult to understand how infants might develop the seeds of rage to then have them sprout into full fledged anger and violence later on in life? Anger seems the natural order of things when the natural order of things is interrupted by a parent's career.

Some parents go to work out of necessity. This is particularly true in one-parent homes. But, many working parents choose career over children for the money, the perks, and the glamour. Only later do they realize that the baby should have come before the BMW, and that they were not home when being home was all that mattered. Ask any teen, from any neighborhood, how often his or her family eats dinner together. You might be saddened by the answer. Some families never eat dinner together. The frozen TV dinners of the 1950s have been replaced by the microwave-ready meals of today.

Adult activities combined with children's academic and sports calendars make togetherness almost impossible. We have placed activities ahead of family unity and society is showing the effects of such a decision. When a pattern of separate lives takes over, the family can only hope to come together occasionally. This pattern exists even with the monied. It has gotten to the point where the only thing family members have in common is a last name.

Adults forget how difficult it is to be an adolescent — the growth spurts with all kinds of hormonal activities and the agony of pimples making teens feel as though small pox scabs are covering their faces as the whole world watches. Into this chaotic mix add sibling rivalry and parental divorce and non-involvement and you have a crazy scheme of things for even the strongest among our children. Growing up can be a painful experience and children need a loving hand to help them through these times. More than ever, teens are now showing the pain of growing up. People speak of the angry faces of children, but can anyone honestly blame them for looking and being angry? It is amazing that they get through anything with all the obstacles present to them.

TV's Nickelodeon channel produced an after-school special entitled *How Divorce Affects Kids*. Hosted by Linda Ellerbee, the program had children talking about divorce instead of the usual adults talking about how they perceive divorce influences children. The main message these 10 to 16 year olds got across was that their divorcing parents needed to be honest with them throughout the break-up of the marriage. In other words, they wanted to feel part of the process as opposed to being left behind to pick-up the pieces.

Adults are surprised to learn how much children understand what is going on in their parents' lives before separation and divorce raise their ugly heads. The children on the panel implored parents to tell them the truth saying that they could handle that better than lies. Their insight can prove extremely helpful in getting other children through what could be the most challenging experience of their young lives.

One of the most painful aspects of today's society is the large number of children being raised in dysfunctional families — the numbers are so large that they are fast becoming the majority. This truth is reflected in the growing number of troubled and emotionally disturbed children in special education classes across the nation. Unfortunately, many emotionally needy children go unidentified and remain within the regular system.

When you mix this large number of emotionally disturbed children with regular education children, one is bound to influence the other. It becomes a numbers game. Children from functional families under the influence of children who have been raised differently, before too long, can be seen altering their way of thinking and acting in order to match the behavior of their dysfunctional classmates. At this point, coming from a completely functional two-parent family is no guarantee that a child will function within normal parameters.

How did the American public school system arrive at this unacceptable state of affairs? What Ray Kerrison called "the national disgrace" in his *New York Post* article[41], continues to be just that. American society has developed, during the second half of the twentieth century, a general disrespect. The family, religion, the law, individual rights, children, fetal life, marriage, fidelity, and standards all have been victims of this growing attitude. People routinely talk to one another in movie theaters. Theatergoers not only dress down, they unashamedly get up and walk out of a play during a live performance. Business deals, once consummated with a handshake, now demand drawn-out legal agreements only to be broken with little concern for the other party.

As for marriage, couples either refuse to enter into it or only do so for religious and cultural reasons with a pre-nuptial agreement. Marriage has become a business deal between two people who are in love, but need to protect their financial assets. Divorce is often an exercise in name calling, and the kidnapping of children away from a spouse or former spouse is epidemic.

The causes for this drastic change in quality of life over the last fifty or sixty years begs to be addressed since several of these causes have a direct impact on our public school education. The gravest and most hurtful cause, of course, has been the dissolution of the family through separation or divorce, and parents, as a result, not being involved in the lives of their children. Other causes worth mentioning are: the discontent the country experienced over the unpopular Vietnam War and the poor treatment of our returning soldiers, POWs, and MIAs by the government, the economic prosperity turned sour, political malcontent on the local, state, and national levels, the assassinations of President Kennedy, his brother, Robert, and Dr. Martin Luther King, Jr., the rampant drug use now in its third generation, and the changing roles of men and women. What society could have withstood all this attack?

Bob Dylan said it best when he sang, "The times they are a'changing." In 1940, the typical school problems were throwing paper, chewing gum, and tardiness to class. Nowadays, drugs, teen alcoholism, teen pregnancy, violence, and suicide are what parents, teachers, and administrators face on a daily basis. All these changes were bound to affect public education since schools are a reflection of the society in which they function. The resultant chaos is real and was predictable.

CHAPTER 2

IMPLICATIONS OF PARENTAL NON-INVOLVEMENT ARE FAR-REACHING

A study carried out in Oregon among junior high school boys aimed to measure the effects of divorce on adolescents. Its findings showed the long-lasting marks divorce left on these children. Further studies showed that these stresses caused children of divorce to have their own children out of wedlock at an unusually high rate. The study made a plea for the two-parent family stating that it was the most stable situation in which to raise a child.

Research by Dr. Wollerstein on *Focus on the Family*[42] found that the trauma of divorce stays with a child through the first three decades of his or her life; a thirty-year effect. As children of divorce grow and form romantic relationships in their late 20's and 30's, the notions of abandonment and separation stay with them. When a couple is considering breaking up, they should think of the long-term effects the divorce will have on the most vulnerable members of the family — the children.

Study after study arrives at the same or very similar conclusion, children need a particular setting in order to grow emotionally, mentally, and physically as healthy human beings. The phase this country has been going through, whereby almost any configuration of family is acceptable, may prove to be a regrettable phase. According to these studies, anything other than a two-parent family is an experiment, but one does not need a study to come to such a conclusion. Common sense tells us that a child needs both a mom and a dad. Situations that differ from this result in trauma and psychological implications. In fact, *Focus On The Family*, an organization from Colorado Springs, Colorado did follow-up studies in 2007 and the results were the same. Divorce has continued at the rate of 55% and so have its resulting consequences. This vicious cycle goes on with a 30 plus year history cutting across our families and our country.

Children of one-parent homes endure pain in various ways. They are needy and have no one to help them sort out the problems of growing up, no one to be a sounding board for the questions that every child must ask during the passage into adulthood. In effect, these children are in a home, but homeless. Admittedly, there are one-parent homes that are loving and nurturing in all the important ways. After all, a harmonious one-parent family is preferable to a two-parent household in discord.

At its worst, the one-parent family is a hostile, restless place from which the street and its dangers become a lure. Children from these homes regularly find solace on the street in all the wrong places. Temptations abound and taboos become invitations. Their language turns vile and the most innocent looking youngsters can lead lives that are less than human. They go searching for someone or something when there is no one available at home. What sadness when that something turns out to be a street gang with all it brings to an easily swayed child.

Children of divorce have usually witnessed all the turmoil that leads to a family's dissolution. They live with the record of those chaotic experiences indelibly printed in their memories. Few separations and divorces are happy matters. As a rule, these break-ups are scarred with accusations and retributions into which the children are inextricably drawn. With that background, children enter an excruciatingly difficult world hostile with drugs, sex, and violence — a world angry at itself.

Children of one-parent families start life at a disadvantage. No matter what single parents say about the quality time they spend with their children, it is nothing like the love of a mom and a dad. There is an evident anger in these children that transcends the usual angst most children experience as they grow up. Children from one-parent families, whether only children or one of several, are different in their frustrated, depressed, let-down state of affairs. There is no surrogate parent, such as a teacher, scout leader, or neighbor who can take the place of a biological parent, no one, no matter how pure and lofty their motives may be.

This discussion does not even begin to address the issue of guilt held by divorcing parents over the dissolution of their marriage and what that dissolution has done to their children and their extended families. The burden of guilt, even when the marriage was destined to fail, is something that must be considered in the body count of modern day divorce in America. It is not only the children we are talking about, parents often suffer gravely, as well.

Adults are victimized by divorce, experiencing the same sense of isolation and loneliness their children feel. News reports have detailed the suffering of divorcing parents when their children become pawns in the revenge play of divorce. A one-parent family produced by divorce is never a win-win situation — everyone suffers to one extent or another.

When husband and wife decide to divorce, we are left with children who feel abandoned. Yes, the one parent has remained, but the pain of the lost parent outweighs the presence of the remaining one. Often, the remaining parent, usually the mother, joins her anger and frustration to that of her children and the sense of abandonment is magnified.

When I was a boy, the only people who got divorced were movie stars. That has definitely changed. An ever-increasing number of people have experienced two or more divorces. Examined collectively, the consciousness of those injured is overwhelmingly charged. Divorce is a disease that infects all those around it; to live in this society is to be affected by it whether you are married, divorced, or single. Our collective consciousness is now geared to separation and that is reflected by the out-of-control incidence of divorce. There is no hesitancy for college graduates, particularly women, to get their first apartment alone and stay there longer than ever before without the thought of marriage. The fear of divorce is, indeed, as far-reaching as its effects.

CHAPTER 3
THE SCHOOL'S APPROACH TO DIVORCE

Public schools approach to divorce has been benign neglect at best since nothing has been done to mediate the effects of divorce on children. Not only are children who come from divorced families the majority, but also many teachers and administrators are divorced as well. The numbers are overwhelming. The fact that schools have not done much in this area, does not mean that much cannot be done.

First, we must examine the general nature of this situation. Tennessee Williams once said that everyone in the world is a romantic.[43] By romantic, he meant that in order to survive one must either love or be loved. If the romantic succeeds in loving and/or being loved, he will survive; if not, he or she will perish. It is a simple enough philosophy that Williams evoked in all his plays. Some of his romantic characters survived and some perished in rather dramatic fashions. What Williams captured in that personal philosophy was a thumb-nail sketch of what life is all about.

We all want someone to hold our hands no matter how old we are. From the child who cries in the middle of the night until a parent comes with a reassuring touch to the elderly patient in a nursing home who longs for a loving hug, we all cry for someone to love us. Just think for a minute of the position a parent holds in the life of a child — all of a child's thoughts, wishes, and dreams orbit around a parent. Understand that no one, absolutely no one, in the entire world can ever take the place of a nurturing mom and dad. Then, try to understand what happens to a child's world when a parent leaves on account of divorce.

The devastating effects of divorce in this country are greater than any bomb an enemy could drop. The long-lasting trauma caused by a parent who leaves can never be assuaged by gifts or quality time given by the remaining parent. We have rocked our children's world by making divorce such a socially acceptable option.

Children of divorce very often act out their anger and frustration through behavioral problems in school. Nowadays, when a child has this kind of problems, the immediate solution is a medical prescription. The consequences of these chemicals, however, are not discussed adequately, and when the subject of side effects like depression or suicide arise in conversation, they are dismissed as rare occurrences. The rare exception is rare as long as it is not your child who becomes an exception, then, all of a sudden, it doesn't seem that rare at all!

Public schools' response to behavioral problems brought about by divorce must be a concerned and sensitive one. Both the home and the school would ideally work together on this campaign and not against each other as they often do in many other areas. The road back to stability for the child of divorce may be difficult, but it is possible. It is the one and only road for us to take as a sane society. Obviously, the road we are currently on is one to further destruction. Our alternative is to have yet another generation enter adulthood without the basic and necessary civilities of life, a life that can be made smoother by some simple, easy-to-follow values.

The one thing that most students in our public schools seem to lack is peace. How can they experience peace, one asks, given the circumstances of modern American life? The faces, words, and actions of our children are hostile. There is no peace in the eyes of our young. We have elementary school children on medication for hyperactivity and we have teens in counseling because of their suicidal tendencies.

Children regularly act out their violence, sometimes with tragic results. They protest the world into which they have been born and are enraged by what they know is a world out of kilter, a world in disharmony. Children know intuitively that the true world is better than what they are being given. Is there any wonder that our public school classrooms are clinics for the emotionally troubled?

We must insert kindness and love into this uneven mix. We must expect schools to adopt what the great leaders of history have always included foremost in their personal pledges — peace. We must direct our children away from responding violently to their sorry states and readjust their ways. We must teach them that there are peaceful ways to settle disputes.

CHAPTER 4

WHAT TO DO FOR THE "DIVORCED" CHILD

What exactly can schools do for children of divorce? Since schools have been asked, in addition to teaching the three Rs, to serve breakfast and lunch, to teach about sex and values, and to be babysitters before school in pre-K programs and after-school in latch-key programs, it is logical to ask them about caring for children whose parents have divorced. Schools have slowly taken on the role of family, but the truth is they do little when it comes to the effects of divorce on children. They have guidance counselors and teams of specialists, but the reality is that schools have had little positive influence on this gigantic social mess.

Our home has historically been our refuge. A place where we could hang our hats in comfort and protection. It has always been *Home Sweet Home* and *Home Is Where The Heart Is*. The home has been the very foundation of our lives. A popular song, *A House Is Not a Home*, reassured us that we needed love to have a real home. The home has been synonymous with love and with all our heart's desires. A good home meant a good life.

The 1950's television show *Father Knows Best*, which portrayed an ideal image of America, was set in a home with a father, a mother, and children. We were shown that life was complete that way. This type of home was archetypal and a good home meant a good child. Adults, including teachers, would often say, "Show me a good home and I'll show you a good student."

Now, that four letter word, home, has taken on a new meaning for many children. Home is a four-letter word because it has become a place where a child finds anger and strife, a place where often only one parent resides, usually just to sleep at the end of a long workday, a place filled with arguments and yelling, a lonely place where the child lets himself in to warm up left-overs and call it dinner.

The only welcoming company to many children nowadays is a TV or a computer through which they can find strangers who instantly become "friends," no matter how unsavory their motives may be. Sometimes, home is a nursery school where adults look after children until 7pm. Far too often, home is no more than a familiar place where children fend for themselves until their parent returns from work. The warm home of yore has been transformed into a cold house.

Under these circumstances, how can we expect children to function properly? What quality of homework gets done when an eleven year old supervises himself? What proper nutrition can be had when children are their own chefs? What acculturation is there for a child who goes from stranger to stranger in school only to be rewarded by an empty house afterwards? For millions of children across this land, the after-school picture is one of aloneness, filled with temptations and no supervision.

The American after-school scenario lacks the nurturing ingredients necessary for children to properly grow emotionally, intellectually, and psychologically. Many teachers have all but given up on receiving completed homework. Much of all reading and written work is routinely done in the classroom. Assigned homework is not even begun in many houses. Would you do your homework when the TV and the Internet beckon? Many adults mistakenly believe that these electronic devices are educational. "They help develop our children's minds," is the argument they use to deny the guilt of having a computer take their place as parents. Denial is their best option because facing the truth would be too painful.

The childhoods of fifty years ago were completely different. What was given to us in the name of love, we can no longer offer to those we love. Parents are ships that cross their children in the night, never able to enjoy each other in the same ways we were able to — with the same exchange of joy. Our children remain unrevealed to us, strangers to those who have given them life.

School functions go unattended and parents rarely go back to school on Back-To-School nights. If they did, many would not be able to discuss their children's study habits, because they don't know them. The tragedy of American life as we enter the twenty-first century is that the solutions to our problems lie with the family, and nobody's home.

In *Home With A Heart* [44], psychologist James Dobson pointed out how children are often ignored in our society. Dr. Dobson observes that the greatest threat to the American family is the over-commitment of husbands and wives to their careers. This "breathless pace" leaves little time for families to be families and, as a result, children are ignored. He sees this as the "quickest route to the destruction of the family." These observations were made over 25 years ago and they remain true today.

Dr. Dobson's is the voice of a sage who has seen way too many well-intentioned families dissolve into divorced parties who communicate through lawyers. Families get caught up in all that society has to offer instead of in each other as families are meant to do.

Some experts advocate for women to stay at home during their children's school years — K-12. It is as important for mothers of teens to be home as it is for mothers of elementary school children, but sadly this is not possible in many American homes. The necessity for both parents to work is often dominant. This "stay at home mother philosophy" is not a popular notion, but it is an important one if we want to positively affect the lives of our children.

There are those who have perceived this madness and have adjusted their lives to a slower pace to accommodate the family as a precious unit. Those who have retreated into the family have gained more than any end-of-year bonus could give — they have gained intimacy with their loved ones. There is a group of New Jersey parents who make a concerted effort to reduce the number of activities they and/or their children attend in order to create more time with and for their families.

Children, particularly boys between the ages of 6 and 11, desperately need a father image in their lives. As a result of a majority of American homes being single-parented, many experience extreme challenges in raising children. In light of the fact that many fathers are either absent or unwilling to contribute emotionally, a male role model must be found by the female parent in charge. An involved grandfather or an emotionally available uncle will often do the trick. If these are missing from the scene, a neighbor or friend might suffice. Whomever it is, a male role model is essential for boys growing up without a father. The degree of harmony that such a male figure brings to a home is not to be discounted. It often brings healing to a mountain of ills caused by a missing father.

In a *New York Post* article from June 3, 2014, Paul Raeburn addresses this very matter. In his book *Do Fathers Matter?*, Raeburn presents studies that show that the death rate of infants whose fathers were not around during pregnancy is nearly four times that of those with engaged dads. Raeburn says that "depression in fathers during their partners' pregnancies — which is more common than most people realize — can increase a child's lifelong risk of delinquency or criminal behavior in adolescents."

In the same article, Raeburn quotes the research of Lynne Vernon-Feagans of the University of North Carolina who found that fathers matter more than mothers. She reported that "fathers made unique contributions to children's language development that went beyond the contributions of education and child care."

The article also talked about how fathers "have a powerful influence on their daughters' sexual behavior during adolescence." In that light, Raeburn makes reference to a 2011 study of Frazer High School in Memphis, Tennessee, that found that one in five female students were either pregnant or had recently given birth. When psychologist Sarah E. Hill of Texas Christian University examined the situation, she found that one in four households was headed by a single mother. Raeburn's article concludes with references to academic studies that state what should perhaps be obvious, "our fathers are important in our lives!"

Girls need good relationships with their fathers to insure good relationships with their future husbands. The lack of a positive male figure sows the seeds of malcontent for both boys and girls. Dana Perino, Presidential Press Secretary to the Bush Family, recently published a book entitled *And The Good News Is* (2015) in which she talks about the important role of the father in the family.

Even *Dear Abby* has gotten into the act of giving advice on educational matters. One of Abby's columns dealt with the theme of values:

Dear Abby: A reader recently asked why we don't have classes in schools to teach kids patience, kindness, manners, not to litter, etc.

Psychologists say that children's personality traits, their ability to get along with others, their perception of right and wrong, their sense of humor, values and morals are formed by age 4. Children are a reflection of their home environment and parental training. Schools should reinforce what the children have already learned.

It's time parents realize that they are the most important 'teachers' in their children's lives. Don't blame the schools. We're doing the best we can.

OLD-FASHIONED TEACHER[45]1

This Old-Fashioned Teacher said it all when she wrote that parents are the most important teachers in their children's lives. To expect strangers, school teachers who are with the children for just so many minutes a day, to develop your child into the perfect being you expect is both ridiculous and unrealistic. But yet, parents regularly hold these expectations of teachers and of schools and are critical when they fail — and fail they must in such an unrealistic role. In fact, how could they possibly succeed? It is easier to blame a faceless institution than to blame ourselves as parents for failing our children.

Unless we return to the notion put forth by the Old-Fashioned Teacher in the *Dear Abby* column, we will continue this exercise in futility, expecting everything from an institution that can at best only reinforce what has already been established at home. The Old-Fashioned Teacher is not old-fashioned at all, just out of mode in an era that has little to go by and few, if any, models to emulate.

We live in a society where people find it easier to leave a challenging situation than to stay and persevere for a solution. The institution where we see this most flagrantly is marriage. Any society that maintains a 55% plus divorce rate over more than a 25 year period is doing something drastically wrong. The human emotional carnage in the wake of this quarter century of emotional slaughter is immeasurable.

The church and the therapy profession have also failed in their attempts to solve society's ills. Throughout the 1970s, 1980s, and 1990s, we heard of a great number of outlandish therapies involving everything from surrogate sexual partners to screaming out loud. This is not to say that the church has not touched the lives of some people and that certain therapies have not been helpful, but overall, both the church and therapy have proven incapable of acting the role of substitute for the family. Again, we need to go home for the solution to our problems, but no one is there.

We live in an era of abundant cruelty in the homes where children are raised. The emotional rape of children, from infancy, is so common it is frightening. By emotional rape, we mean a household where arguing, physical abuse, and name-calling are the norm and where children don't get to know the hugs and kisses of a loving mother and father. How about the number of children who routinely witness their mothers being abused? And the equally alarming number of children who witness violent verbal arguments between their parents?

Part of a child's basic temperament is his or her value system. A value system, like a language, cannot be inherited through genes. A value system is something children learn from the moment of birth and is as telling as the color of their hair. Parents and other adults teach through the way they act in the presence of their children — what a child sees, a child does.

The question of spending quality time with their children brings up all kinds of guilt with separated or divorced parents, as well as with parents who live together but are constantly being pulled away by work requirements and leisure-time pursuits. Are you really with your children when you are with them? Are you giving your children your undivided attention or are you with them physically, but not emotionally?

One parent proudly told me that he takes his children to the movies every Sunday afternoon. What he neglected to mention was that the kids went into one theater at the multiplex and he went into another. After both movies ended, he would gather his children and take them home. It appeared as though they had spent the afternoon together, but in reality they had not shared anything, not even the popcorn.

Another parent bragged how he always spent his evenings at home with his children, but the truth was that he spent them in the living room watching TV while his children were in their rooms on their computers. True, they were all home, but they were in separate sections of the house doing their own thing. The only sharing took place at 10 pm when the children came out to bid their Dad a good night.

Kids cannot be fooled. No matter what parents say about the subject, children clearly know if their parents are involved and caring. Being in the physical presence of your children is an important step, but it is only the first step. Getting into the emotional and social presence of your children is what creates quality involvement.

There are psychologists and philosophers who believe that a difficult and trying life filled with exasperating experiences gives character and strength to a person's life. Of course, there are others who believe that this type of life makes you crazy. To those who hold to the character and strength theory, our present crop of children ought to be ready for anything later in life. Many have had such devastatingly adverse backgrounds that we can only pray and hope for the best.

As a nation, we have withdrawn our energy from the home, but through our love for one another, homes can be revived, nourished, and re-instated as the centerpieces of our culture. Once that happens, the problems we see elsewhere in our society will be reduced and then eliminated. If every head of household assumes rightful responsibility for what goes on in the family, our houses can once again be turned into homes.

SECTION IV

THE OUTSIDE WORLD AND THE PUBLIC SCHOOL

CHAPTER 1

THE PRESENCE OF SEX, VIOLENCE, AND DRUGS IN PUBLIC SCHOOLS

Growing up in 1950's America, the greatest fear you had was of contracting polio, but Dr. Jonas Salk took care of that fear. In those days, schools were mild and the notion of violence within a school was unheard of. Kids took temper tantrums to school, not knives and guns. Gum chewing and an addiction to Rock N' Roll were the biggest concerns in the classroom. Teachers were extensions of the parents. A teacher's word was the law, never questioned, always revered. Parents usually went beyond a teacher's punishment to demonstrate their support for her and what *she* held high. Yes, the teacher was always a *she* since it was a woman's profession at the time.

Situations from the 1950's, reflected in TV shows like *Ozzie and Harriet*, are laughed at today. Today, polio is a disease from history books and our fears have been taken over by AIDS, STDs, and e-bola. The modern home looks nothing like Ozzie and Harriet's. Suppertime scenes from that show are foreign to families now. Now, few families have dinner together — no one is home for that.

The dinner table was the place where many problems were solved in the American homes of bygone days. Now, problems fester as teens nuke dinner and have TVs, computers, and cellphones as dinner companions. The head of the household often works late and/or the children have after-school activities. Almost everything takes the place of the family at dinnertime. No matter what they are, what they cost, or what they produce, parents' and children's ever present after-school activities are destructive to the root and core of America. How can we expect children to learn how to make decisions and face the difficulties of growing up without the council of experience and love?

There are real concerns in present society that deal with life and death situations. At one time, if a child was a half-hour late, there was no reason for alarm. Nowadays, an overdue child is reason enough to call the police. At one time, neighbors were extensions of the family. Now, few people know their neighbors. "Don't talk to strangers," is the abiding principle in our neighborhoods where distrust prevails.

The evening news reported a case where a boy, who had been physically assaulted by another boy, was taken to the hospital where he lost his life. The hospital personnel spent six hours tracking down the dead boy's parents in order to deliver the heartbreaking news. No one knew where they were, not even the boy's brother and sister. This is not an isolated case now, but it would have been unheard of years ago.

I know a 16-year old boy who eats dinner every night in front of his computer in his bedroom with the blessing of his single-parent mother. There is no dinner-time discussion about the course of his day. The boy had insisted on this arrangement and the mother gave in to his demand. This, too, is not an isolated case. As you might imagine, this young man has developed anti-social behaviors and doesn't know how to interact with other people. His behavior is odd, and is being condoned by his own mother.

One of the most disturbing aspects of modern-day schools is the degree of violence that prevails. This violence goes far beyond the occasional fist fight, this is life and death violence. In 1996, New York City spent over $7 million to correct the problem of violence[46] — this number is small in today's budget.

It is routine for high schools in large cities to have armed, uniformed, city policemen patrolling the corridors and securing the entrances. In many cases, middle schools have also found it necessary to hire armed policemen. Metal detectors and front door intercom systems are now routine. Consider that for a moment, we have to have metal detectors at the entrances to our schools. These have now become the normal and accepted scenarios nationwide. We have given in to school violence and allow our children to be housed in police/military camps during the daytime. Imagine having to subject children to a metal detector search as they enter the building every morning!

News reports of students bringing guns to school and killing their teachers and fellow students are now commonplace. These cases have been chronicled, explored, analyzed, and dissected, but school-gun-violence keeps on happening. The lethal combination of children, guns, and schools is one contemporary phenomenon that we must strive to conquer.

Crime in and around schools has reached such a fever pitch that many schools have implemented a zero tolerance policy on weapons, serious assaults, and drugs. This is especially necessary in areas where gangs rule our inner-city high schools. Belmont High in Los Angeles, often referred to as *Horror High* by insiders, was populated by no less that 54 in-house gangs in the 1990s, all sporting their own colors and hand signals for communicating. Many decent, honest teens are forced to join gangs for reasons of protection alone. And, what about the teachers who have to teach in this environment? They and the staff are subjected to the same police/military encampment as the students. Is it possible to teach and learn under these conditions?

This hostile climate is engendered by a lack of respect and civility. *Public Agenda* found "high levels of concern about disruptive students and a lack of discipline and order in public schools." Whereas "7 in 10 teens say there are too many disruptive students in their school," only 13% of public school students say their classmates are "very respectful" of their teachers.[47] The report found that the issue of respect transcended racial and ethnic boundaries. A war, if you will, has begun pitting students against teachers and gangs against gangs. The results of this tension are violence and death. The *Public Agenda* made an important point in the mid-1990s:

> Given the broad societal concern about a lack of civility and social cohesion, and declining moral values, it should not surprise us that these issues emerge at school. And, although students often describe a lack of respect between teachers and students, they saved some of their harshest criticism for selected classmates. Many teens described a rough-edged

and threatening environment — with problems ranging from cliques to guns to drugs.[48]

Schools reflect the popularization of guns as a means of solving problems in our society. Wrapped up in all this discord is the acceptability of cheating as a way of life in schools and colleges. Surveys show that a majority of students see nothing wrong with cheating as a way to get better grades. Honesty and integrity are no longer valued. Students know that cheating is wrong, but since everyone does it, why bother being honest in a dishonest environment? This attitude is a social issue of huge dimensions.

More than ever, schools and homes need to develop a cooperative relationship. If we had a magic wand that we could wave over the land and cause illegal drugs to disappear, we would experience the equally magical results of a drug-free society. In that one instant, 7 of 10 arrests in large cities like New York would be unnecessary. Police would be bumping into one another instead of scrambling to cover large case loads. Hundreds of billions of dollars could be re-routed to areas in need, or equally appealing, taxes could be reduced. Emotional and psychological tensions would also lessen. The successful elimination of drugs in our society would bring about a new renaissance. This one area of crime has that much power and influence on the way we live, on our streets, and on our schools.

No school district escapes violence and valueless behavior. Even educationally upper-echelon school systems have introduced programs to teach students proper behavior in and out of school. *The Social Competency Program*, developed at Wellesley College in Massachusetts, offers teachers two lessons per week that they can infuse into the curriculum; these range from proper classroom decorum to resolving playground disputes. Teachers in Massachusetts school districts are encouraged to present monthly workshops to parents in order to insure that the same values are reinforced at home. Exclusive suburbs are no longer that exclusive due to the continuous stream of violence and profanity being channeled into our homes via television and the Internet. No one is immune to negative role models and vulgar behavior.

Near the Thanksgiving holidays of 1997 in the rural town of West Paducah, Kentucky, a 14-year-old ninth grader shot and killed several students who were meeting early one morning in the local high school as part of a Christian prayer group. The boy entered and emptied his .22 caliber gun of all its bullets. When the unprovoked, senseless act was over, three of his fellow students lay dead. Asked by authorities for a motive, the boy could give no explanation, appearing as though he had been caught in the middle of a minor offense. The boy did not have a history of violence. He was what his classmates called a typical, quiet boy, friendly and not thought of as troubled. What had been a quiet Kentucky town the day before, became the front page headline in newspapers around the world.

No one needs to be reminded of the violence experienced in Newtown, CT where 20 students and 6 teachers were shot dead on December 12, 2012. Since that time, there have been over 100 more shootings in schools nationwide. We must accept the fact that no school is safe from gun violence, and yet, there is no national outcry in support of gun control and the eradication of gun violence in schools.

A video that went viral in January 2015 showed a high school student at John F. Kennedy High School in Paterson, New Jersey knocking down his 62 year old science teacher when the teacher attempted to take the teenager's cell phone from him during class. It went viral because so many people find violence intolerable. More unbelievably, that video has been followed by innumerable others showing teachers physically assaulted and verbally abused **inside the classroom.** This would have been incredible at one time in our history, now it has become commonplace in our schools. Students video the assaults and post them online with a sense of righteousness and immunity. The public no longer feels that teachers, administrators, and school boards are capable of assuring student safety and of providing a secure environment for their children.

The story of New York public school health and physical education teacher Ray Ramirez speaks volumes on the condition of inner-city schools. On a brisk, autumn day, Mr. Ramirez noticed a boy who had entered the school building illegally. He approached him and asked if he belonged in the school. At this, the boy became verbally abusive and threatened the teacher with bodily harm. Mr. Ramirez ordered him to leave the building and the boy began trash talking. At this point, Mr. Ramirez went to a hall phone to call the Dean of Discipline for assistance. Suddenly, he felt himself being held by another student as the first boy started to punch him in the face, head, and body. Mr. Ramirez was beaten so badly that he needed hospital treatment for his wounds and was detained for fear of a possible concussion to the head in addition to being treated for shock.

When Mr. Ramirez attempted to file charges against the boy who attacked him, he was informed that it would be next to impossible to have charges brought against him because the boy was a special education student and that placed him under the protective mantel of the courts. Not only was the teacher angry and bitter at this, but he was frightened to return to work for fear of reprisals from his assailant. On account of the many acts of violence in and around New York City public schools in the 1990s, Mayor Rudolph Giuliani ordered that there should be at least one police officer in each of the city's high schools. Imagine that!

The incident of teacher Ray Ramirez had multiple impact — depending on the audience. It sent a message of lawlessness to the community, a message of fear to teachers and well-behaved students, and most importantly, a message of complacency to administrators and politicians who are in charge. It is as though society is saying, "Do anything you want and you'll be OK." Shakespeare stated it best when he had Lady Macduff say the following lines in the tragic story of *Macbeth*:

> I am in this earthly world, where to do harm
> Is often laudable, to do good sometime
> Accounted dangerous folly.[49]

At one time, teachers chose to remain in their classrooms until well after their hair had turned gray. Now, the practice of "25 years and out" is common and eagerly anticipated by many in the teaching profession. In fact, many school systems have buy-out plans that offer financial incentives for earlier retirement than that allowed by the State law. Public school teaching is no longer a life-long job.

We support this nonsense by allowing the wrong people to inhabit and control the corridors, classrooms, and cafeterias of our schools. Enough stories of violence against teachers and students have made the headlines; it is long overdue that justice prevails in our schools. In buildings where democracy, the Bill of Rights, and the Constitution are taught in the classrooms, violence and drugs rule the lavatories, cafeterias, and gymnasiums.

In a 1994 *Public Agenda* study entitled *First Things First: What Americans Expect from the Public Schools*[50] it was revealed that the public held a "disturbing new fear, that the schools are violent and unsafe." This is not news to those of us in public school education. We see students and teachers threatened and assaulted on a daily basis with lukewarm reaction from the judicial system. The *Public Agenda* report went on to elaborate that participants in their survey listed three images which summarize their feelings that public schools have failed: "metal detectors in high schools, students smoking outside schools during school hours, and supermarket checkout clerks who can't make change."[51]

Those surveyed in *First Things First* cried out for safety, order, and the basics; a call repeated many times throughout the country by people who believe that our schools are not providing the basic foundation for education. In fact, as long ago as 1994, a Gallup Poll showed that Americans most frequently list violence and discipline problems as their greatest concerns in public schools.

We are at the point where even parents admit that they are not doing a good job in disciplining their children. The problem has reached that nadir of impossibility. During the 1990's, we became focused on preventing violence and lack of order in our schools. Now, more than two decades later, we are convinced that things have only gotten worse. Violence has overtaken our nation's public schools.

In the early 1980's, Paterson, New Jersey's East Side High School was overrun with violence, drugs, extortion, and prostitution. It took a hard-nosed principal named Joe Clark to turn things around. Mr. Clark, the inspiration for the film *Lean On Me*, baseball bat and megaphone in hand would patrol the halls of East Side High. He met with many who tried to obstruct him. He represented change and change is an ordeal no matter if it takes a positive or a negative form. He got tough with students and teachers and demanded a no-nonsense, academic climate within his school. Mr. Clark had been an obscure elementary school Vice Principal before being transferred to East Side High and given the chance to head a corrupt high school within 20 miles of the New York metropolitan area. He was intent on doing the right thing, and he did.

Within a few years of Mr. Clark's appointment, the school had been turned around. He was cited on television talk shows and featured on the cover of *Time* magazine for his tough approach in solving the ills of our urban schools. Mr. Clark was effective because he established the foundation of a sound school: safety, order, and the basics. He fought violent students, hostile teachers, and politically corrupt School Board Trustees in his quest to right the wrongs that befell East Side High. Through his actions, Joe Clark demonstrated that with the right amount of care, it is possible to rescue a school from even the most hopeless situation. Unfortunately, his energy and determination are rare among public school administrators, especially now.

Teen gangs have also taken our schools by storm. In New York City, the Latin Kings are such a presence that they were featured on WABC's *Prime Time* hosted by Diane Sawyer. The then New York Police Commissioner Safir called them a group of "dangerous thugs" who rule the streets with violence. This gang has invaded many of the city's schools, turning school property into gang turf. *Prime Time* showed gang members presenting themselves as part of a religion called Kingism, but their lifestyles suggested something other than religion. The feature ended with Ms. Sawyer reporting that the leader of the Latin Kings, King Tone, had been arrested and charged with domestic violence.

This violent street mentality uses threats, physical beatings and, in some cases, even death to silence those who oppose it. This is the reality of the cultural milieu in which many of our children grow. Surprisingly, many of these youths take part in gang activities with their parents' full knowledge and cooperation. The justification being that it is safer to be part of a gang since they protect their own.

An act that wounded the very soul of humanity took place in Jonesboro, Arkansas in March 1998. An eleven year old and his thirteen year old friend pulled a fire alarm at the Westside Middle School and, armed with high-powered rifles and hundreds of rounds of bullets, waited in the woods for the students and teachers to exit the building. The boys then opened fire killing four students and a teacher. The reason? One of the killer boys was angry at a girl for breaking up with him.

It is not the fault of public school education that there is violence in schools or that students involve themselves in drugs and pre-marital sex. It is not the fault of public school education that more children than ever come from one-parent homes and bring social problems with them to school every day. But in the end, schools are still faced with solving all these challenges.

An increasing number of children, ages 5 to 7, are taking Prozac. Add to this the already established teen population on the drug, and you have an alarming amount of young people taking medication to get through the day. Depression, a malady usually associated with stressed-out adults, is the cause for most of these prescriptions being written. Prozac, Ritalin, and street drugs are affecting a growing number of our children.

Learning experts have recently estimated that up to 20% of all students may have a learning disability in the form of a neurological deficit ranging from mild to severe. These learning disabilities make it difficult for children to read and write. When you add this learning disadvantage to the existing problems of alcohol, drugs, sex, one-parent families, violence on television, movies, music and violent video games, you end up with a perfect storm that places many children in peril of failing before they even begin high school.

The situation is desperate in some New Jersey school districts. So desperate that a Recovery High School program was established in 2014 by New Jersey State Senator Raymond Lesniak (D-Union). The purpose of the Recovery High School is to serve students suffering from substance-abuse by providing an environment in which they can be free of the dangers of illegal substances. There, in addition to their regularly scheduled courses, they receive counseling to help them conquer their addictions. The goal is to establish Recovery High Schools across the nation to respond to the needs of students in danger of losing their lives through addiction and crime. Drug addicted teens are epidemic in number, and for many of them, attending their regularly scheduled schools is a dangerous mistake since it implies being in close proximity to familiar "sellers" who will stop at nothing to keep them hooked on drugs.

The documentary *Race To Nowhere* challenges current thinking about how we prepare our children for success. It chronicles heartbreaking stories of students across the country who have been pushed to the brink by over-scheduling, over-testing, and the relentless pressure to achieve. The film points to a silent epidemic in our schools. Through the testimony of educators, parents, and experts in education, it reveals an education system in which cheating has become commonplace, students have become disengaged, stress-related illness, depression, and burnout are rampant, and young people arrive in college and/or the workplace unprepared and uninspired.

Rosemarie Bello-Hornak knows well what is going on inside inner-city public schools. An experienced R.N. with a speciality in midwifery, she is currently involved with a large group of inner-city girls, ages 11 to 21, as a consultant and mentor. These young ladies regularly meet Mrs. Hornak at a medical clinic she administers inside a large urban hospital. Wanting to keep things informal, Rosemarie asks them to call her one of several names: mid-wife Ro, Miss Ro, or just Ro. She wants the girls to feel welcome to trust her with their sexual concerns.

When you first meet Rosemarie Hornak, you are taken with her joy and positive attitude about life. On a daily basis, she witnesses the lives of these sexually active young women and explains, "No one does the dance anymore, they just do it." Young women have sex without the desire or need for any courtship or romance. Sex for the sake of sex is what is happening in our inner-cities.

The younger girls in her group receive training with menstrual issues and regular gynecological check-ups. Many of the older girls are already actively involved with intercourse in addition to oral sex, which also forms a big and frequent part of these girls' sexual lives. Hornak explains that oral sex brings gratification to the boys and allows girls to remain attractive, plus it takes care of the fear of pregnancy. According to Mrs. Hornak, "there is an incredible amount of sexual activity taking place in the lives of these girls."

Part of the unspoken contract she has with the girls is that she will not share the girls' sexual activities with their mothers. That "contract" is the foundation of the trust they feel towards her; without it, there would be little ability to reach the girls at this vulnerable stage — trust is essential.

Rosemarie feels that the large-scale promiscuity among pre-teen and teen-age girls is mostly due to broken families and the lack of father figures in the house. She estimates that 90% of the girls in her clinic are from broken homes. This, in turn, causes the girls to feel a nearly complete lack of self-esteem and self-confidence. She added that technology also plays a role in facilitating the girls' situation with cell phones causing children to grow up too fast and giving them instant access to their friends and hook ups. Rosemarie warns her girls that "a little 'hook-up' can cause irreparable damage for the rest of their lives." Her main lesson is abstinence, and abstinence is the goal she encourages her girls to follow.

Rosemarie reasons that this is "not just sex, it is low self-esteem causing this promiscuous behavior, which, in turn, has caused the wide-spread sexually transmitted infections (STI)." Because certain diseases such as gonorrhea can be treated with drugs, they no longer pose the fear they once did. Now, the dangers lurking in the streets and back seats of cars where young people gather for sex are herpes, HIV, HPV, and hepatitis. These viruses become a permanent part of a person's DNA. The symptoms can be treated, but the virus will always be present.

The lack of parental involvement is obvious. In these girls' cases, a medical clinic, no matter how good, cannot fill the place of a dutiful parent; an institution is no parent at all. Children, both boys and girls, are in desperate need of guidance. The family is the best and perhaps the only place where self-esteem, self-love, and abstinence can be taught. Often, the best teacher is setting a good example. Young women tend to fashion themselves after the women nearest them, a mother, an aunt, an older sister, a teacher, a neighbor, or a friend can potentially serve as models for impressionable young girls. Lacking this, they will turn to film, television, or music personalities to try to find direction and meaning in what it means to be a woman in contemporary society and how one should behave.

CHAPTER 2

THE INFLUENCE OF TV, MOVIES, VIDEO GAMES, MUSIC, CELL PHONES AND THE INTERNET ON SCHOOL CHILDREN

During the late 1990s, Dr. James Dobson, the popular, nationally syndicated, radio psychologist, shared some very telling facts about television usage among youths aged 9 to 17. He reported that 42% of children and teens in that age group had cable TV in their bedrooms. An alarming percentage when you realize that this highly impressionable age group has unlimited access to uncensored sex and violence in their very own rooms.

In another day and age, television watching was a family activity that took place in American living rooms. There was no cable television nor was there sex, violence, or nudity on the airwaves. Today, in 21st century America, children watch television and surf the net while alone and unsupervised.

In a June 2015 *WSJ* article, Jennifer Breheny Wallace reported that "recent studies suggest that viewing media as a family can still be a great way to bond." She goes on to write, "Sixty years ago, television served as a center of family home life. Today, the average American owns four digital devices on which to consume media." Back then, we had three networks, "now the average home has 189 channels to choose from."

Sixty years ago, according to Ms. Wallace, "shared activities led to greater levels of personal disclosure for adolescent boys, more positive family functioning for adolescent girls and greater parental involvement for both." Times have changed and so have family patterns. She also found that "99% of TV episodes contained some form of adult content, like sex, violence or profanity." The article concluded by saying that "Families want shows that are 'safe' to watch together, and they're not getting them on today's broadcast television."

Parents have no idea what their easily swayed children are watching. Television and computers have become magical babysitters that keep children quietly occupied for hours. After years of this digital influence, the child that emerges from the bedroom is "suddenly" as unrecognizable to the parents as an alien from another planet would be.

Would you as a parent welcome a stranger who rang the bell and asked to play alone with your child in his or her bedroom? Would you welcome a child molester or a drug pusher into your child's bedroom? How comfortable would you feel with allowing such a person in your home? Newton Minow, the former Chairman of the FCC, asked a similar question in an interview, and found that any intelligent parent would bar the door against such an intruder and immediately dial 911 for emergency help. No parent would knowingly invite a corrupting influence into his or her children's lives. Right? The truth, however, is that parents regularly allow potential criminal influences into the lives of their children by allowing hours of unsupervised television watching and computer usage. Being quiet in his or her bedroom does not mean that the child is safe or protected. Being quiet in the bedroom warrants a look at what is going on there. Parents may be surprised to learn the answer to that.

Often, there is no adult available to censor the questionable pictures, language, nudity, violence, and glorification of criminals. Who bought the television set or the computer? Who allowed them in the privacy of a child's bedroom? Who pays the cable and internet bills? Who suffers the heartache of having their children become less than what they hoped?

Just as we have done, we can undo. It is not too late. Is it ever too late to rescue a child? Children crave structure and care. They would want to be told how much and what to watch on television. The good, old-fashioned family conversation may not be as frequent as it once was, but it will never be out of style. Your child would love for you to inquire about his interests, wants, wishes, fears, questions, and opinions. They want you to be present and listen to them.

A recent survey on the habits of children was seeking to discover how children aged 11 to 18 spend their time out of school? "Out of school time" was defined as leisure time when the youngster was home. The results showed that our children spend as much as 11 hours a week watching television. This is just an average because many parents report that their children watch many more hours. We also need to take into consideration the fact that computers have taken the place of television in many children's lives, so, when looked on average, 11 hours of TV a week is a great deal of TV viewing.

Other findings suggested that 10 hours a week go to listening to the radio and CDs, and 6 ½ hours a week are spent on the phone. That is nearly 28 hours a week in front of the television, listening to music, and/or talking on the phone. Further down the totem pole of out-of-school leisure time activities are time with friends (they've talked to them on the phone), doing chores around the house, and looking through magazines.

We often talk about how computers have changed our lives, but let's look at how it has changed the lives of our children. More and more time is spent in front of a computer screen than playing outside. Cell phones are hand-held computers and most children have smart phones of their own. In making these devices so readily available to children, we have given them carte blanche to the world; the good and the bad alike. Computers and cell phones are addictive. They can easily hijack our attention for hours and this is without mentioning video games — another source of distraction along with their violent and often disturbing content.

Children quickly learn about virtual meeting places and share this information with one another. Some of these sites can provide wonderful educational experiences, but others are outright dangerous, especially for children. Computers are tools, neutral instruments; good and evil reside in the users' minds.

We shape and encourage our children's habits by what we allow, and we are allowing them to use productive tools in non-productive, harmful ways. Our consciences makes us buy them the best computer we can afford thinking that we are doing a great justice by acquiring a state of the art electronic educational machine, but what really determines the machine's educational value is the parents' close supervision and direction. What appears to be the act of a loving parent in support of a child's education, can turn out to be a $2,000 plus investment in keeping the child busy with inane activities and fully abreast of the latest trends in porn and social dysfunctions.

Do we continue to allow this nonsense in our homes and in the minds of our children? Or, do we put a stop to it and replaced it with something worthwhile? As adults, we need to demand better instead of acting as though we are helpless when it comes to raising and educating our children. Expect more and you will receive more. We would explode in anger if we saw someone trying to negatively influence our children, and yet we condone the same negativity when it comes in the form of a television program or a computer blog. By allowing this, we are allowing our children's morals and values to be dictated by strangers on a screen — no wonder so many teens already have sexually active lives. It is time to take full and complete responsibility for our children.

Another element parents need to consider in establishing a decency code for their children is the strong influence and pull that peer pressure can exert. Peer pressure under the influence of the entertainment industry can lead to all kinds of behavior and experimentation, sexually and otherwise. Parents need to band together if they are to turn the tide we are currently riding and demand better quality media for their children.

Our children are casualties of the war for our entertainment dollars. They are never quite the same after accepting violence, sex, and obscenity into their lives. The age of innocence is short-lived in America. We take our youths from nursery rhymes to the realities of divorce and dysfunctional domestic behavior in the course of a few short years. What have we done to our children's innocence?

There are no laws preventing nudity, profanity, explicit sexual dialogue, and violence from entering our homes. Child porn has gone high-tech. Discussions are taking place to restrict these areas, but they are only discussions. In the name of free speech, we continue to allow and develop technology that holds within its midst a cesspool of vulgarity with criminal minds surfing the web looking for lonely and impressionable children upon whom they can prey.

There have been numerous news stories of children who have been persuaded to run away by people they met on the Internet. What the news fails to report is the number of children who stay home, but leave behind any semblance of values when they become taken with the trash they hear from total strangers over their computers. There is no news story that can ever capture the sense of morality that has been lost.

Freedom of speech takes on a different timbre when your children are exposed to offensive material. Freedom of speech is something else when a stranger buys a bus ticket for your child and convinces him or her to leave the state for what turns out to be a sexual encounter. Freedom of speech is violated when your child is engaged in sexual conversations online. Freedom of speech becomes victimization when the Internet and the sexually violent language it contains injures your child.

It is now commonplace for schools to have Internet service in every classroom and make it available to children as young as those in the primary grades. Of course, no school official wants a child to be offended with material on the web and there is no school that installs this expensive equipment with the intent of harming its students, but along with useful learning material, the Internet contains violent and sexual content which makes the purchase of additional software necessary in order to prohibit users from accessing sexually explicit pages.

Such a simple act of a flick of the switch seems to be difficult for most. To monitor television viewing, a parent has to be aware of what is on the television. Even a simple scanning of the television listing would give a parent an excellent idea of what is good TV viewing and what is not. It almost sounds like an old-fashioned idea to have parents watch television with their children, and it is, but some old-fashioned ideas are the best ideas.

Developments in television programming over the last few years have brought an adult tone to what used to be wholesome prime time television, and children can now watch television anywhere they please without supervision of any kind. If parents are watchful over computer habits, kids can watch whatever they like on their cellphones and/or tablets. Basically, as long as a child has a cellphone, which they all seem to have, there is no possible way for parents to monitor content.

An ancillary problem develops with this scenario, the problem of separation and alienation. As a result of this "independent" behavior, families no longer discuss what they watch on television, since it is highly improbable that they are watching the same shows. What are parents to do?!

The *Wall Street Journal*[2] printed an article by Lee Siegel entitled *America the Vulgar* that talked about the widespread coarseness in American pop culture. The writer is quick to point out that sex screams out in all aspects of our culture; from TV shows to Internet images, children and adults alike are exposed to sex in an "endless stream of solicitations."

Mr. Siegel asks the obvious question, "When did the culture become so coarse?" He considers himself a sophisticated man of the day, but laments that there is no longer sexual innuendo — explicit sex is everywhere. He goes on to say, "subtlety stimulates the imagination, while casual obscenity drowns it out." The article mention Elvis' gyrations and the Rolling Stones lyrics of an earlier day, but feels they were "calibrated to the times;" a tease to the culture of those days.

Mr. Siegel makes a poignant point in outlining the "JFK assassination, the bloody rampage of Charles Manson . . . the incredible violence of the Vietnam War – shocking history in the making that was once hidden now became visible in American living rooms and bedrooms night after night, through new technology, TV in particular." The Vietnam War was the first military conflict to play out directly in our homes through television. He points out that "Culture raced to catch up with the straightforward transcriptions of current events."

The article goes on to say that "The Internet and pornography go together" well and that the lowest impulses often shape our cultural norms. He can only hope that the pendulum will one day swing the other way. We can only hope there will be relief from the casual coarseness and vulgarity enveloping our society.

We live in an electronically addicted society. Cell phones are a marvelous invention. Through their use, we now have the ability to instantly connect with everyone in the world. They have brought us GPS guidance, texting, and instant answers to our questions via the various search engines. Cell phones are hand held miracles that have changed our relationship to one another and to the world, but, unfortunately, they have become an obsession, and an obsession by definition is something that takes over our lives — an addiction. Cell phone addiction, ironically, has drastically reduced our ability to communicate person-to-person. We are in touch with one another electronically, but not in a face-to-face, emotional way.

A few years ago, Oprah Winfrey had several shows dedicated to the topic of cell phones. She could see, for example, the danger that calling and texting presented to both the motoring public and to pedestrians. The Fort Lee, New Jersey police quickly began to enforce a j-walking violation for all pedestrians using their electronic devices when crossing the street. The first day of enforcement saw 70 tickets issued in the city's two square miles.

Sadly, the issuing of tickets is accomplishing little in preventing people from walking and driving while using their devices. This is one of those social crimes that are not easily stopped by the law. Only the development of social awareness, as Winfrey intended, will help create a consciousness in which such senseless activities become history. As it stands now, talking or texting while driving is only a secondary offense in most states necessitating you to be stopped for another violation before you can be charged with a crime associated with cell phone use. The cell phone lobby in Washington, D.C. and in state capitals around the country has proven quite strong and effective!

Our addiction to cell phones has become an accepted part of our mores. Society doesn't seem aware enough to even question the ways in which this advancement in technology will affect our lives in the long run. Cell phones are here to stay and we have all jumped on the bandwagon. Recently, I observed a three-year old toddler playing with a plastic cell phone. When asked, the mother's simple answer was that they were getting their child ready for her first real one by having her practice on the toy.

"What do we do?," you may be asking. What we must never do is give up on the situation; too many before us have given up which explains the present state of affairs. First, we must demand that television and the Internet immediately stop the transmission of negative values. We must get to know our children's habits and try our best to monitor their movie going and television watching. Observe what they watch. Read film reviews and support citizen groups who argue for decency in the entertainment industry. Accept nothing less than what is acceptable.

We all intuitively know the influences that will hurt our children. No parent needs a censor to tell him or her what is worthy of viewing. Do the homework. Listen to the music your children listen to no matter how painful it may be to your ears and sensibilities. Listen carefully, and voice a loud resounding "no" to companies that put out questionable material by refusing to buy it and/or sponsor it in any way. Remember, it is parents who empower their children. Take your power back by buying only quality material that will serve to entertain and educate in ways that agree with your values. Make a distinction between freedom of speech and abuse and vulgarity.

This posture takes energy and it takes work, but the effort is worth all the trouble since it is your children's minds and souls that are at stake. Let your local, state, and federal legislators know about your disapproval and demand that you are represented properly by having them question the industry as to why they release products that are harmful to children. When challenged by freedom of speech, counter with the fact that your children do not deserve to be emotionally assaulted by obscene language and pornographic images. Obscenity and pornography don't represent freedom of any kind, but are rather an assault on your children.

Television shows, online videos, and films corrupt our children on a daily basis with their harmful content. Adults must assume responsibility for what is happening since they are the ones who open the door and allow this filthy material into their children's minds.

CHAPTER 3
THE INFLUENCE OF THE NEWS ON SCHOOL CHILDREN

Jack Valenti had a richly woven career in politics and motion pictures. During a 38 year period, he presided over the Motion Picture Association of America and, prior to that, in the 1960's, he had been Special Assistant to President Lyndon B. Johnson. In the winter of 1997, Mr. Valenti gave a fascinating talk at the University of Arkansas in which he stated that we then had more than 2,000 hours a day of television, if you included the expanding cable networks. A staggering amount of images projected 24 hours a day, seven days a week, 365 days a year. Television was never off in America.

Jack Valenti was also the creator of the motion picture rating system which, with minor changes, continues today. He felt there was an "abandonment of children" on the part of parents who bring or allow their children to attend R rated movies. In an analogy similar to Mr. Minow from the FCC, Valenti asked if people would give their children poison. He likened children's attendance at R rated films with violence, sex, and profane language, to feeding your children poison for dinner. He cited the slogan of TV news as being "if it bleeds, it leads" and saddened in the current state of television news coverage. All this took place in 1997, 20 years ago, and what was true then is even worse now. We all lose in the media environment we have created for ourselves. We lose our humanity as we support this destructive climate. It is up to us to demand changes.

On July 26, 1998, the President of the United States received a subpoena to answer sexual misconduct charges. Bill Clinton was the first American President to testify as a defendant in a court case and the legacy of his tenure in office has been tainted by the dark cloud of the Paula Jones and Monica Lewinsky accusations. Consider the situation for a moment: the President of the United States is accused of soliciting a state employee for sexual favors while he was governor of Arkansas. If you believe the accuser's story, she was requested to go to his hotel room for what she believed was a job opportunity, but the opportunity for a job faded in the passion of the moment when things allegedly turned to lust. As to the Monica Lewinsky case, it was alleged that the intern had engaged in sexual activities with President Clinton in the Oval Office.

Believing one side over the other is irrelevant. The astonishing point is that the leader of our country, the commander of the military forces, the man who holds the position that every boy and girl in the country covets, the personification of all that is wise and just, the man to whom we look when disaster occurs, the most powerful man in the world was accused of sexual misconduct and the scandal has lingered for this many years.

Forty-two years ago, president Richard Nixon was forced to resign during his second term in office over his involvement in the Watergate scandal. For allegations that many judged more severe, Bill Clinton continued to enjoy an enviable popularity until his last days in office. The public was willing to dismiss the sexual misconduct charges as long as the economy remained stable. In the years since, President Clinton continues to enjoy great popularity and commands a six-figure speaking fee. All this has, of course, been digested through the Internet and television to our children. Do we ever stop to think the kind of message this sends to our children?

Years from now, when historians look back on this era, they will record it as a tormented time of political and financial unrest and of down-spiraling values. In this negative mix, we find our children watching, listening, and feeling everything around them. Nothing passes by the keen observation of a child. Our families are disjointed, our economy is shaky, violence seems to permeate from all sources of entertainment, and drugs continue to be the motivation behind many crimes. Maybe it was because of all this confusion in our society that we didn't get more upset by the charges against Bill Clinton but, whatever the cause of our complacency, we are teaching our children a silent lesson.

The endless stories of police corruption are certainly part of this confusion. Sworn to uphold the law, policemen have long been looked upon as the protectors of young and old. Recently, a radio newscast reported that five police departments within a 20-mile radius were under Federal investigation for corruption within the ranks. One was alleged to have connections to the Cuban Mafia in promoting drugs and prostitution and another has been charged with operating a burglary ring within the department — policemen would case a house for valuables and then would break in through a back window and rob the place. This went on for several years involving police superiors as well as patrolmen.

The five police departments in question were located in two different New Jersey counties not far from New York City. It appeared for a while that part of a police department's work was to operate in criminal activities — a disturbingly negative message to young, impressionable children and teens. At the very least, a youngster would come away with a jaundiced eye regarding the police. No longer would these children look upon a policeman or the police department in the same way; this news had to go far in destroying values in their minds.

News of this kind tend to incriminate all police in the public's mind. As unfair as it may be, it is the psychology that follows this type of events. Now, the uniformed men on the streets become suspicious. During the Winter of 2014-2015, New York City's mayor, Bill de Blasio, stated publicly that he had instructed his bi-racial son to be wary of the police!

The latest phenomenon is the daily reports of criminal athletes. Reports that tell us, in unasked for detail, the latest crimes our athlete-heroes have added to their resumes. Be it drugs, robbery, or rape, we are sure to learn all the grisly facts that will go to destroy yet another mythical figure. How many times do we need to see beloved professional athletes in handcuffs being escorted out of nightclubs at 4 am?

We see an NBA star attempt to murder his coach. We learn how the NFL is doing its best to turn a convicted sex offender and woman abuser into an altar boy, even sending him out to high schools on free speaking engagements. A so-called world champion bites his challenger's ear when he gets behind in the fight — this millionaire's excuse, "I have children to support and didn't want to lose the bout." This dethroned chump, I mean champ, was paid $8 million in his loss.

The problem is not that this frequently takes place, but that we believe the excuses offered by these thugs who inhabit the highest ranks of collegiate and pro sports. How about the number of players who hold long histories of violence on women? We turn them into heroes through ignoring criminal behavior that, in another time, would have been their ticket to oblivion. Now, it is their ticket to the Pro-Bowl. In spite of all this, we must remember that just as we have created this topsy-turvy world, we can re-create a world filled with harmonious elements and people.

It is not uncommon for parents of elementary and intermediate school students to drive their children to school and pick them up every day. Sometimes, the imaginary fears of parents become so real that they *expect* something to happen to their children. In some of their minds, it is a foregone conclusion that junior will be a casualty, in some form or another, of the wars going on in and around the school building.

Add to these unfavorable circumstances the perceptions of adults about children and you become even more concerned. In a *Public Agenda* survey some startling feelings were revealed. Six in ten adults surveyed were "deeply troubled by the character and values exhibited by young people today."[53] The concerns these adults held were in the areas of honesty, respect, and responsibility. The fears went further to the morals our children display. In the same study, 67% used words such as rude, impossible, and wild to describe teens. Only 12% of those surveyed used terms such as smart or helpful. In the discussion focus groups following the survey, one man said, "There is anger inside of them." It is exactly that anger that erupts in the classrooms, halls, cafeterias, and playgrounds of our schools.

Going beyond the historical distrust that an older generation sometimes feels for its youth, these adults have a deep intuition of the demeanor and behavior of teens, and they are concerned. When only 1 in 8 adults finds teenagers respectful and friendly, we are beyond any sense of traditional distrust. One of the most interesting aspects about this study is that the parents of teens agree with the findings. You would think that parents might be more protective, but only 12% of those asked would define teens as friendly and helpful.

The next logical question then is, "What to do?" The public calls for schools to teach morals and values, and many states have taken on that debate. The real issue, though, is in determining where we have gone wrong in teaching these fundamentals. If the public looks upon morals and values as a vaccine against the ills and dangers of society, why haven't the children been given their shots at home? Or, if they have been given their shots, has the vaccine been too weak? Once again, the truth of the matter is that there is no one at home to administer them. This vaccine is one that must be issued on a daily basis from birth through young adulthood by the child's family.

Instead of their parents, contemporary children model strangers whether in daycare or in the form of babysitters, nannies, and entertainment personalities. These strangers pass on their morals and values to our impressionable children. To have the schools teach values is as ludicrous as having them be responsible for breakfast, lunch, and sex education. Twenty-five years ago, Americans became unable to give their children the essentials of life such as nourishment, knowledge of intimate behavior, morals and values, and they now expect a cold, strange institution to take on the highly personal responsibility of raising their children.

Public Agenda made the eye-opening discovery in *Kids These Days: What Americans Think About the Next Generation* that the public is upset with the behavior of children and teens. The study defined children as "those older than five but not yet in their teens." Those questioned find that children have become "spoiled kids" who are "mindlessly acquisitive, mini-consumers who demand, and get, electronic gadgets and designer clothes and sneakers, things they have come to expect as a matter of right."[54]

When over 90% of adults questioned say that it is a widespread value failure, a force of equal proportion is necessary for us to combat this at a national level. Americans no longer look to the next generation as being better than the present one, and the source of children as our greatest national asset is now in serious question. America's children are no longer an asset, but a growing liability.

We live in a plea bargaining society where few, adults or children, are held accountable for their actions. When we listen to television news or read the newspapers, we see the unfolding history of a society that does not want to point the finger of accusation. Time and again, we hear of hardened criminals caught red-handed being charged with a lesser crime or, in too many cases, being let off on a technicality.

Isn't it time to realize that the liberal ways of legal pundits have not worked to the benefit of society as a whole? Any child that is not punished the first time he is caught cheating will not think twice about cheating again. The excuse of not enough prisons is not an excuse. The excuse of a reformed criminal has proven invalid enough times to make the idea of parole seem harmful.

Since the late 1980s, physicians and psychologists have been reporting cases of children and teens mutilating themselves. In fact, experts called self-mutilation the addiction of the 1990s. What a telling act! Self-mutilation indicates self-hatred of such intensity that the mutilator wants to assist in his own destruction. Cutting and burning one's own body are the most common forms of self-mutilation.

We live in a country that worships youth; a point brought home by the majority of television and magazine advertisements. Look closely at television programming and you'll see a youthful audience as the target. This idolization of youth in the West is radically different from the Eastern viewpoint where age equals wisdom. In America, you are a throwaway bottle once you pass the age of 30, while in the East, you have not reached maturity at that age. We can't wait to send our elderly to nursing homes, while in the East, they are placed at the head of the table as wise family advisers.

In what intellectual, emotional, and physical condition do we find today's youth? If all indications are correct, the prognosis for this generation is not good. In fact, it is frightening. Through so much neglect, our children are rudderless ships on a stormy sea, Titanics headed for fatal icebergs. As adults, our duty must be to chart a better course for them.

At this stage, we need to chart *a* course, since none is apparent. All these areas of concern, intellectual, emotional, and physical, need adult supervision, but we need to go home to get direction. Our youth need to be our priority, not in a commercial advertising sense, but in a loving, caring, nurturing sense. These elements have been missing from our youth for the last few generations. It is not too late to add this ingredient to the all-important mix of life; it is never too late.

CHAPTER 4

THE TEACHING OF VALUES
IN THE SCHOOLS

One point of agreement between the general public and most public school teachers is that values such as honesty, responsibility, and respect should be taught. They also agree that tolerance and harmony among people ought to be part of the values curriculum. In fact, teaching values was very much the apple pie of the 1990s in public school education. After all, who would have the audacity to oppose good 'ol American values?

This kind of thinking is rubbish. How can anyone teach golden values in public schools while sex, violence, and drugs are so widely and attractively presented by the media. Sex, violence, and drugs are the "in" thing. In a society of questionable values, what we say is very different from what we do. Researchers can research all they want and come up with all kinds of evidence, but it is all for nothing when our lifestyles are determined by what sells and not by what is right. What sells? Sex, violence, and drugs!

Until we collectively decide to end the hypocrisy and do the right thing, the mixed message will continue to flow. We aim to teach our children good, wholesome values and morals, but then show the opposite through our TV and Internet choices. If our actions don't match our words there is no hope for the current situation to change.

It is difficult to distinguish the parents from the children inside many homes. America is populated by households where children are the boss ruling the roost with an iron tongue. In these emotionally dysfunctional homes, parents have given up on discipline by giving in to their children's demands. They mistakenly believe that it is easier to give in than to assert their values. Giving in is never the answer. Parents do not have to be despots or rule with an iron hand, but they need to realize that they are the sculptors of their children's lives and not the other way around. Parents must set the example.

A pediatrician friend tells an unbelievable story about one of her six-year-old patients and the way she reigned over her parents. Late one night, the parents called to report symptoms, one of which was fever. The pediatrician asked them how they knew the child had a fever and the parents responded that the baby's head felt warm. The physician then asked the parents to confirm the presence of fever by taking the girl's temperature, but the parents responded that the child would not allow them to do so. A six-year old would not allow the probe to be placed in her ear to measure her temperature. The child had already made clear her independence from parental control.

Parenting and discipline begin at birth. To have a child refuse medical intervention is absurd, but unfortunately, it happens too often. If a six-year old can lay claim to such power over two adults, what is she capable of doing when she reaches the ages of 10 or 15? Perhaps she'll be the one setting curfew for her parents. The way most Americans go about raising their children is lopsided and unexplainable. Discipline intermixed with love is the only recipe. It must begin at birth and continue throughout the child's life with support for the fair discipline administered in school.

The Federal Government is seen as an enemy of the people and as the institution one tries to cheat in order to get a break on taxes or a tax refund at the end of the fiscal year. Cheating is a regular habit on income tax preparation. Neighbors are not neighbors anymore. We fear each other. The further from your neighbor the better. Years ago, people living in the same neighborhood or city tenement building knew one another and would look after one another's children on the streets. The adults in a neighborhood were parents to the neighborhood children, whether they were biologically related or not. Nowadays, the disciplining of a child by an adult other than the parent would be cause for a law suit.

Immigrants presently entering the country are also of a different mentality than those who entered America at the beginning of the twentieth century. At that time, America was an opportunity given and received thankfully by the largely peasant men and women. There was a special humility about the immigration experience and a life of celebration when citizenship was granted. Today, some immigrants have an attitude of expected privilege and entitlement. Many take a "you owe me" stance as they come through our ports *demanding* liberty. In many cases, the immigrant hand is no longer extended in request for entrance, but is raised in a fist demanding power.

Experts conservatively estimate that between 12 and 20 million illegal immigrants have come through our borders from Mexico. If that number is correct, the effect it may have on the United States government and its citizens could be staggering. Furthermore, officials in Washington are presenting bills that would allow undocumented, illegal aliens to have the right of citizenship and the privilege to vote. It seems, standards for American citizenship are no longer required.

Times have changed so much in these last 50 years that this country is almost unrecognizable. It is time to get back into harmony. It is essential for us to return to a state of life where people trust themselves, each other, and the world around them. We have to go back to the values of the past to insure our future.

If government has failed to improve the lives of our children and homes are unoccupied and/or unable to offer a solution to their problems, then the only alternative left would be the schools. But, according to a *Public Agenda*[55] poll, the public believes that schools have abandoned their roles of reinforcing "responsibility, integrity, and respect." This leaves us in a hopeless situation. Time and again, public opinion surveys show that people believe schools should "teach values along with academics." Race does not appear to make a difference when it comes to the public's perception of what is wrong with our schools and how to fix them. The public has little or no confidence in politicians' ability to help whether at a federal, state, county, or local levels — any poll can give evidence to this.

The public expects schools to do the much needed job of teaching values, and educators, on the other hand, expect parents to teach these lessons. No one will enter the dance floor under these circumstances, so children will continue to define their codes of ethics from movies, television, and the Internet — not an optimistic picture.

A number of NFL players have made headlines with the domestic violence they demonstrate. More notably, Baltimore Ravens player Ray Rice was video-taped beating his girlfriend in an elevator — they have since been married! This incident led to all sorts of denials on the part of the NFL and its commissioner as to their knowledge of the domestic abuse. Our so-called heroes' behavior is much less than heroic and continuously disappoints with its lack of character. Because of the high esteem so many of our youths have for these personalities, it is not unusual for them to defend their role models' illegal behavior. This is hero worship gone wrong with children finding nothing improper with activities that have nothing right about them. But, who else would they worship when these hoodlums and thugs are praised by all and sundry?

This is a case of misdirected youth. Children are willing to follow the right path, but have no one to show it to them. We all need a map or compass when in the wilderness of decision-making. Children are routinely given the wrong map and a compass pointing towards destruction. This is the generation that needs to be taught values in school since they are not learning them at home.

The question of role models often comes up in discussions about school children. In the 1950s, we had a great deal of positive role models from whom children could take direction, but when a national survey finds that only 1 in 5 Americans (22%) say, "It's very common to find parents who are good role models for their kids," one must ask, who are the modern-day role models? Film characters that use violence as a means to an end? Promiscuous rock stars? You can take your pick. Many films associate sex with violence, sometimes treating them as one and the same — a great mes-sage for our children! Television movies are even worse since they bring the negative messages directly into the home.

Much of modern music has also joined the violent-sexual-obscene-crude-angry scene. These are the drugs we daily feed our children helping them grow into "healthy" angry and violent adults. This formula is a simple equation that we all can understand. We get from our children what we put into them — gar-bage in, garbage out.

If we love our children, it is time we have them associate with positive role models that inspire and educate. The choice and the power are fully ours, not Hollywood's or the record industry's. Hollywood and the music industry work for us, so let them work *for* us. Let's fire negative influences and hire positive role models. Can we blame anyone but ourselves if we don't?

The most difficult step is always the first one because it requires the greatest amount of expended energy. Halting this moving locomotive might not be easy, but it is possible. It will take one parent at a time creating a powerful chain across the nation. It is never easy to say "no" to a child, particularly for single parents, but those "nos" will help turn the tide on the absurdity that we have allowed into our society and are currently experiencing.

Whenever it is said that the responsibility is ours, it is met with resistance. Character is a word we use rather often and having good character is something we desire for ourselves and certainly for our children. But, good character is built on a code of ethics and morals; it does not come out of thin air. Adults demonstrate their codes of ethics through their behavior and manners. Religion makes ethics and morals a sacrament and tells us there is punishment in the hereafter for not following the straight and narrow road as outlined. We must be taught ethics and morals somewhere. The fact that schools are now being mandated to teach values is a declaration that we have failed. Particularly disappointing is the failure of religion to stem the tide against a questionably ethical and almost immoral flood in our society.

The topic of respect doesn't come up very often in conversation, largely because it no longer exists. Notice how we treat one another. Take a seat in a public place and watch what happens. Actually, little happens because people now interact less than ever spending the majority of their time staring into cellphones and tablets. People regularly walk in front of one another, step in doorways ahead of others, and race for taxi door handles to the chagrin of a slower-moving person. Our treatment of one another is utterly disrespectful.

This behavior would be bad enough if it were limited to adults, but it is not. Sit quietly in a school cafeteria or playground and watch how children interact with one another. Take note of the manner of speech they use and, even more importantly, their tone. Children speak to one another with disdain in a rude manner. Their speech reflecting both their anger at an unfriendly world and their lack of social etiquette. Children are no longer taught to say "thank you" and "please." By the time they arrive at school, this ingrained behavior is difficult to root out. For a certain segment, manners are something foreign since they are not perceived as necessary in a world that rewards the strong. Manners are not associated with strength, but with those who are weak. What a huge mistake it is to assume that politeness indicates anything but strength and civility. Children are not only often rude and vulgar, but their use of obscenities has become commonplace.

Asian countries revere the elderly and usually seat them at the head of the table. In many cultures, gray hair is a sign of wisdom and not uselessness as it is here in America. In Asia, adult children would never think of making an important decision without consulting an older parent. In fact, many Asian companies have a senior adviser on staff to lend the wisdom of his years to any and all business decisions.

Peace and harmony are desperately missing from the public school education system and from society as a whole. That lack is reflected in the behavior and language of students and in the fact that so many states are mandating values education in their schools. Parents and teachers all over complain about the deplorable manners of children. Parents experiencing it with their own and teachers with all kinds of students no matter their social or economic backgrounds.

The way we dress is another indicator of how we think about ourselves and the world around us. Our dress has become casual to the point of being sloppy. Rarely do we dress up to go out to dinner at restaurants that once demanded a dress code. Most high school boys not only don't know how to knot a tie, they don't even own one. They never find themselves in a social setting that calls for a tie. Life has become so casual that an *entire generation* is completely unaccustomed to wearing a suit. This type of dress code was unimaginable in the past.

Teachers decided years ago to get so casual in their dress that many have become indistinguishable from students. It is not uncommon for teachers to wear jeans to class on a regular basis. Many Boards of Education have found it necessary to implement dress codes for their teachers. Can you imagine a Board of Education having to write a policy of dress for the professionals it has hired? Do you suppose that students will dress properly if their teachers don't?

Children are often broken by the time they enter school and, as time goes by, continue to be broken by the experiences of life. How can a reform movement that will correct the issues of the family, especially of a one-parent family be incorporated in schools? The lack of food in the stomachs of millions of youngsters has been addressed at the cost of billions of dollars through breakfast and lunch programs. The problem of what to do with these youngsters after schools close at 3pm has been corrected by leaving the schools open until 7pm with latch-key babysitting, again at a very expensive price. We address the rampant use of drugs by adding drug education to health classes. Largely, drug and sex education is an attempt to make up for the inefficient family, but it does not work — the school is not, and never will be, the family. Families must teach ethics and values so that drugs and promiscuous sex stop being so attractive to their children. Families have to stop looking outside for the prevention and correction of problems that are only solvable from within.

The fundamental problems faced by education are of a social nature and must be addressed at that level in order to be solved successfully. We are currently expending our resources in a direction that will bring little return, if any. The results of our labors have been thus far frustration magnified.

One of the most serious dilemmas now faced by our children is that of self-image. As a result of living in an environment filled with violence, sex, drugs, and alcohol, and devoid of values, children don't know who they are. In 2013, the U.S. Department of Justice reported that there were 1,000 cases of domestic violence every day in this country. Mass media tells children that they are part of this take-all-you-can world mentality while moral education, if taught at home and in church, tells them quite the opposite. The media's message is taking the day and, as a consequence, you'll see children and teenagers who, for example, emulate prison inmates and criminals in their attire. You'll also see schools that allow that sort of dress, largely because the officials are unable and unwilling to do anything about it.

The drug culture, with its drive-by shootings and gang mentality, has become more and more attractive to children from good families because the parents have allowed this negative influence to enter their homes. As we have seen, the infection comes directly, electronically, and digitally into our children. Children engage in sex at a stage in their lives when the last thing they need is a sexual experience. They act out anti-family and anti-school episodes when they need the family and school the most. Once promising children and teens show all the earmarks of suicide, the ultimate lack-of-promise attitude that a human can experience.

Mix the influence of violence, sex, drugs, and alcohol into a test tube filled with one-parent families, add even a small amount of negativity, and the result will be hopelessness in the spirit of a wonderfully pure child. We have been allowing this to go on for years now. In the name of free speech, our television sets and Internet continue to pour the most offensive messages into our children's consciousness. This is too high a price to pay. If the results of this experiment are consistently disastrous for our children, why do we insist on repeating the same pathological patterns?

No matter what survey groups conduct questionnaires to determine the public opinion on educational issues, the reality is that our society's standards have decayed. In spite of the proliferation of pre-K schools throughout the country, children no longer arrive in kindergarten versed in the basic ABCs. Pre-K schools are really institutional babysitters so parents can re-enter the labor force sooner. Strangers are now caring for and teaching children at a time when parents ought to be carrying out these responsibilities. This makes an enormous difference in children's lives.

During the elementary school years, over 50% of children will go through the trauma of a parent leaving — usually the father. During elementary school, children will also learn about drugs, fear of strangers, AIDS, and have concerns about sex. A bit too much to place on the shoulders of a little child. Failure in such an environment is almost expected.

Why have the two sides in this dispute split into opposing camps? Confusion and disagreement often precede a successful outcome. There is a revolution in education and the battle lines are clearly drawn. As a matter of fact, the battle has already begun. Anytime there is a question of morals and values, a lack of or total absence of discipline in the home is being indicated. When parents can't or won't discipline there is chaos, and in today's American family, they seem to be either unwilling or unable to do so. In the modern home, discipline has become "do what you want, get what you demand, and answer only to yourself without fear of retribution."

We have gotten so far from where we need to be that the journey back to balance may be a difficult one that will meet with strong resistance. But, this trip back home is the only one we can take, the only viable option. This time, the trip is one of life and death. If we don't return home soon, the way may be completely lost.

SECTION V

HOPEFUL EXAMPLES FOR NEW TEACHERS AND STYLES OF TEACHING

CHARTER SCHOOLS

Parents are malcontent with public schools and now that there are other options like charter and private schools, they are looking elsewhere to educate their children, supporting charter schools in particular. The entire charter school system was created to compensate for the fact that too many parents and students were disappointed in their neighborhoods' public schools. Charter schools looked to fill the educational void and were a direct response to the failing public school system.

In an attempt to understand the rising number of charter schools, I visited the Elysian Charter School of Hoboken, New Jersey. The school's director is Dr. Harry Laub, a seasoned administrator who is proud of his school and its students' accomplishments.

Elysian was founded in 1997 and has an enrollment of 288 students chosen through a lottery held each January. It has an average class size of 16 students, a big plus for any school. According to Dr. Laub, the most important difference between Elysian and other Hoboken public schools is that it offers parents a choice of progressive and community building education, oriented towards project work, problem solving, and innovative ways of learning. For example, Elysian students do not sit in desks. Instead, they sit at tables where the focus is on team work. Dr. Laub considers Elysian his dream school and enthuses, "What we are doing works!"

At Elysian, the staff and the board of trustees are fully committed to progressive education. The school's climate is uplifting and energetically positive. Dr. Laub guided me on a tour of the school where I observed highly motivated students with faces full of enthusiasm hard at work on classroom projects.

I asked Dr. Laub what he would say to parents who asked why they should send their children to Elysian Charter and without hesitation he responded, "We are a school that focuses on the growth of each individual child, not only academically, but also socially and emotionally. Our classrooms are structured to represent real world situations in which children learn to problem solve issues both individually and as a team. Skills learning, which is carefully planned, is an outgrowth of these projects. We also develop a warm and nurturing atmosphere that is conducive to taking the risks that support learning."

During my visit, I was introduced to some of the teachers, and observed students both in the classrooms and out in the halls. After a lifetime in public school education, I concluded that what the Elysian Charter School offers is an intelligent and hugely viable alternative to the public school experience.

As of this writing, there are approximately 6,000 charter schools nationwide; 6% of the total public elementary, middle, and high schools in the country. But, most noteworthy, charter schools are popping all over the country in increasing numbers every year.

In New York City, a grand example of the emerging charter school is the Success Academy founded by former New York City councilwoman Eva S. Moschovitz in 2006. Ms. Moschovitz now has 32 schools in 4 of the 5 boroughs, multiple elementary schools and one high school. Success Academy plans to open an additional high school as the students in the elementary schools mature. Ms. Moschovitz's goal is to establish 100 charter schools throughout the city. These schools, primarily in poor black and hispanic neighborhoods, have already begun to outscore public schools in wealthy suburbs. Last year, New York City public schools showed 29% of their students passing reading and 35% passing math state tests, whereas Success Academy showed 64% passing in reading and a whopping 94% passing in math.

What does Success Academy have that other public schools do not? It is devoted to accountability, not only from their students, but also from teachers. It has explicit rules and precise expectations. Students wear uniforms; the girls wear jumpers and the boys shirts and ties. The way a student dresses determines the way a student behaves.

Another element that stands out about Success Academy is that teachers are not unionized and many are just out of college and eager to do well. There is a high teacher turn-over rate, though, because the day for a Success Academy teacher is long and many beginning teachers do not adhere to such long work days when they are paid comparably to teachers in other public schools.

Also worthy of mention is that all Success Academy middle school students receive iPads and are instructed in their use. In 2013, Success Academy received approximately $72 million in public funds and $22 million in donations.

Ms. Moskowitz believes that "structure and consistency leads to better outcomes." At present, Success Academy has an enrollment of 9,000 students, and this year alone there were 22,000 applications for 2,688 vacant seats. The schools are showing a high percentage in both attracting and keeping their students.

Success Academy schools are built around critical thinking and tailored to the individual scholar's needs. The schools place a particular emphasis on reading, since "A love of reading leads to a lifetime of learning which is key to success in college and beyond." There is also focus on children becoming "good citizens." "Respect for others and proper behavior are explicitly taught, modeled, expected, and rewarded." Furthermore, "Values and strong moral character are a part of (their) daily instruction, starting in pre-K." At Success Academy, they "help children learn the value of setting goals and making a strong effort, of 'going beyond' to get the job done."

As the Elysian Charter and Success Academy prove, there are successful alternatives to the current, failing public school system. There are students who want to learn and teachers who want to teach unhampered by politics that prevent real progress. There are people in other urban areas either already doing what Success Academy does or getting ready to do so. It is impossible to prevent the human spirit from expressing itself. These two schools as well as many others around the country embody this every day.

FAMOUS PEOPLE PROGRAM

While working at the Palisades Park School System in New Jersey, I launched a program called *The Famous People Program*. Beginning in 1979, it came about in a most interesting way. One day, a student asked if I wanted her cousin to come to the school and meet the students. Her cousin was Jeff Weston, a player for the New York Giants. What I liked most about Jeff, more than him being a player for the Giants, was that he was a graduate of Notre Dame University, so I immediately accepted the opportunity.

Jeff came in and addressed an 11th grade class of 20 English students in a classroom setting. He was a gigantic hit! The students were in awe of this first class athlete and his imposing 6' 5", 235 pound muscled physique. After he left, the students were abuzz that a Giant football player had visited. The excitement was palpable throughout the school even though Jeff had only appeared in one English class.

A month later, I read in the local newspaper that the Miss New Jersey contestant in the *Miss USA* beauty pageant lived only a few miles away from our school. I wrote her a letter with only her name and town as address, and Patty La Terra received it, accepted the invitation, and came to our school. When she arrived, I wondered as to how she had gotten my letter. She looked at me, smiled, and said, "Dr. Muciaccia, my father is the postmaster of West New York, where I live." If things are supposed to happen, they happen.

The day Patty La Terra came to the school, she was shadowed by several TV and newspaper reporters. One of them asked to interview me by saying, "Dr. Muciaccia, last month you had Jeff Weston of the Giants and today you have Patty LaTerra. What is it that you have here?" I looked to the heavens above, then into his eyes, and said, "this is *The Famous People Program*, created for the purpose of showing students that 'Nothing Beats Determination' and 'Hard Work Equals Success.'" That was the beginning of what turned out to be a 21-year program that hosted 180 guests from all walks of life.

Other guests included Alec Baldwin, Harry Connick, Jr., several Yankees, more Giant football players, anchors from most of the New York City television news shows including Rosanna Scotto, who currently co-hosts a morning show on FOX 5 in New York City, broadway performers, elected officials, and Detective Steve McDonald of the NYPD who was shot in Central Park by a bicycle thief and was left paralyzed.

DEREK JETER

In the midst of all the violence and negative publicity among professional athletes, there is the story of Derek Jeter who played twenty consecutive seasons for the New York Yankees. As a boy in the Little League, young Derek's dream was to play shortstop for the Yankees, and he was able to live that dream to the fullest.

Derek Jeter is a role model for children of all ages. His career was marked by an absence of scandal and an abundant amount of respect both for himself and for everyone with whom he played. Derek was consistently in the spotlight for his sportsmanship, and before his retirement, he established the *Turn 2 Foundation* to help needy children. The foundation continues with a reputation of honesty, integrity, and sound fiscal responsibility.

There are men and women in professional athletics in this country who still are positive role models and deserving of our respect. Sadly, the media jumps mostly on negative stories because they sell. The NFL, under close scrutiny lately, also has many men of high quality, as does the NBA, but we seldom hear about them. Good, charitable acts don't generate the same value for media outlets that a good, salacious scandal does.

GIANLUCA DIMUCCIO

Gianluca DiMuccio is an extraordinary man who, within a fourteen year period, rose from school janitor to principal. His story is one of determination, hard work, passion and, most of all, love for his students.

At the age of 22, Gianluca found himself a college graduate in need of work. To help make ends meet, he took a job mopping floors and emptying wastepaper baskets in a New York State school that housed students with disabilities. He took the janitorial job as a temporary solution, since his goal was to head out to California and pursue a career in theatre, his college major. He was in for the surprise of his life. Somewhere along the way, Gianluca fell in love with the school's special needs students and his feelings were so strong and genuine that he went right back to school to become certified in teaching the developmentally disabled.

Although he refers to his journey from the janitor's closet to the principal's office as kismet, the road was paved with the passion he developed for special needs education. With love as his foundation, he was guaranteed success.

His first step was to become a teacher's assistant. When the opportunity presented itself, he immediately seized it so he could have direct access to the students and start learning how to better help them. He returned to school, earned a master's degree in special education from the City College of New York, and by the fall of 2005, Gianluca was a full fledged teacher of developmentally disadvantaged children. The thoughts of going to California had been completely forgotten.

Gianluca's teaching philosophy is "having the ability to see greatness in each student." During our interview, he related stories of several students with the passion of a man in love with his job. His students are fortunate to have him as their teacher.

The children in his care have been diagnosed with cognitive, physical, and mental disabilities. Gianluca feels that his role is not only to help them, but also their families. The children experience a wide-range of disorders including brain tumors, autism, Down's syndrome, seizures, and mental fragility. Gianluca "learned how to be a real human being by working with these kids," and says that the love of what he does is why he does it.

Gianluca's own background is part of the reason he loves his career. The son of Italian immigrants, he was born and raised in The Bronx, New York. Having grown up in an Italian speaking household, he had noticeable problems speaking English and was placed in special education classes. Kids at school were mean to him making him feel like he didn't belong. His only safe haven was the nurse's office where Miss Oates would nurture him like a loving, surrogate mother. Gianluca says that having to overcome fear changed his life. It made him realize that there is greatness on the other side and that nothing is too big to overcome.

A teacher of the developmentally disadvantaged since 2005, by 2014, he was curriculum coordinator, and a year later, he became assistant principal with a staff of 220 and a student enrollment of 270. In the Summer of 2016, he was appointed principal of the school where he had once mopped floors.

A tattoo on the inside of Gianluca's forearm reads "Don't let anybody steal your peace" — a lesson borne out of his childhood experiences. He also believes that "comparison is the thief of joy." As a janitor, he was intimidated by some of the teachers, but that intimidation did not prevent him from being respectful towards everyone — students, teachers, and parents. Now, as principal, he views people with the same respect he had while rising up the career ladder. Gianluca feels that "if you give respect, you get it back" and that "all work, no matter how humble, is important."

The tale of ascending from janitor to school principal sounds fantastical, but Gianluca Di Muccio made it possible with focus, determination and, most importantly, love for himself and his profession.

JACK MOOK

We need to emphasize good deeds and de-emphasize the violence that takes place in our society. Pittsburgh police detective Jack Mook exemplifies what I mean. Detective Mook is a 46-year old, 22-year veteran of the Pittsburg Police Department, a former paratrooper, and a Desert Storm veteran. He volunteers for an after-school program at the Steel City Boxing Gym teaching boys the sport of boxing. In addition to all this, he is also someone who carried out an extraordinary act of love.

Detective Mook had taught brothers Josh and Jesse through the boxing program for several months, until, one day, the boys failed to appear at the gym. After several weeks of their absence, Detective Mook became concerned and suspicious. Using his skills as a detective, he discovered the brothers were living in a foster home under deplorable conditions. They were in foster care because their biological parents were drug addicted and unable to care for them.

The foster parents in this case turned out to be worse than the biological parents. Detective Mook, not the type to stand idle in the face of human need, got child services to allow him to foster 16 year old Josh and 12 year old Jesse, and then filed adoption papers to legally adopted the brothers as his own. Josh and Jesse are now Mooks!

Jack Mook had every reason to leave Josh and Jesse in "the system," but chose not to. Instead, he made the life-altering decision to become their father. The brothers love this arrangement and so does Detective Mook.

The Mooks' story teaches us what we can do for others and how in doing for others we, ultimately, do for ourselves. By enriching Josh and Jesse's lives, Jack Mook has enriched his own. Since adopting the brothers, Detective Mook married his sweetheart and now, a wonderful family is at the heart of Josh and Jesse's lives.

Detective Jack Mook touched the soul of mankind by lifting up these two beautiful boys. Through his actions, he teaches us the most important lesson of all — the power of love to open the doors to happiness and success!

PAMELA DRUCKERMAN'S "FRENCH BEBE"

While some Americans anguish over parenthood, French parents are raising happy, well-behaved children without any of the drama American parents experience. In 2012, Pamela Druckerman wrote a book entitled *Bringing Up Bebe* offering positive strategies we can apply to raising children. Pamela, an American mother living in France with her British husband, noticed that French children were much better behaved than their American counterparts — particularly during dinner time. Whether in restaurants or at home, she observed that French children would sit quietly in their high chairs. During endless hours spent in French playgrounds, Mrs. Druckerman never witnessed a French child throw a temper tantrum. In fact, the only playground temper tantrums she witnessed while living in France were thrown by her own children!

According to Mrs. Druckerman, the French manage to be involved with their families without becoming obsessive. She observed that French parents, unlike Americans, were not at the constant service of their children. In her observation, Americans are "over-parenting or hyper-parenting." The French have a "whole different framework for raising kids," perhaps it is one that America might profit by adopting.

One of the keys to the French parenting success is that they teach children the simple act of learning how to wait. French parents don't pick up their children the second they start crying. Another successful strategy is that they don't allow children to snack all day like American children. French children have been taught to wait until dinner time to eat. They are also taught to play by themselves, to be independent and, as a result, they learn to be happy by themselves.

The lessons Mrs. Druckerman learned in raising children by watching the French model include: delay gratification, teach them how to happily play by themselves, teach them to be happy being by themselves, and speak to your children in a tone of voice that has conviction.

Isn't it possible for Americans to apply these strategies in raising our children? Can we drop our arrogance and look to other cultures for new ideas? We can learn much from the French model and, perhaps, from other cultural models as well since ours is desperately calling out for a revision and/or an update.

ST. BENEDICT'S PREP

In the Spring of 2016, *60 Minutes* broadcast a segment on St. Benedict's Prep, a nearly 150 year old school in Newark, New Jersey. Scott Pelley covered the story and did a wonderful job presenting St. Benedict's Prep to the viewing audience. I decided to include St. Benedict's Prep in this book to show that schools can succeed, even under the worst conditions, if genuine love for the students exists.

Newark, New Jersey has been in dire straits for the last fifty years. Its situation has not improved much since the 1967 riots when residents attempted to burn down the city. In 2015, there were 111 murders, one third of the adult population lived below the poverty level, and the unemployment level was consistently above 10%. In order to interview St. Benedict Prep's headmaster, Father Edwin D. Leahy O.S.B., I chose to walk from the train station in downtown Newark to the school, a distance of approximately 15 blocks. As I walked through the center of Newark, I saw hundreds of employable men and women just standing on street corners.

St. Benedict's Prep is out of place in some regards. Some have called it an "oasis" and it appears to be just that in the middle of Newark. SBP includes grades 7 through 12. There are 550 students in attendance, 65 of whom live on campus because they are either homeless or their homes are so unsafe that SBP represents the only safety in their lives. The school has become their home.

Meeting Father Ed was a breath of fresh air on a hot, stuffy day. He has been the school's headmaster for the last 40 years. A 1963 graduate of SBP, Father Ed recalls the specific moment during his school days when he knew he would spend the rest of his life there. He even remembers the spot on campus where that feeling overcame him. SBP is his school. There is even a building on campus named *Leahy House* where the 65 boys who live at the school are housed.

Father Ed belongs to the Newark Abbey of St. Benedict. A straight-forward man of much faith and determination, he is tall and his posture reflects who he is and what he stands for. But, not all is sweet and rosy, there are times when Father Ed must practice tough love towards the students and he is not afraid to do so.

SBP is guided by *The Rule*, an edict established by St. Benedict in the 6th century. Following *The Rule*, students are allowed to run the school themselves. In doing so, they are heard, have influence, and can create an atmosphere of success both in their academics and in their lives.

To enter SBP, candidates usually need to pass an entrance exam, but some exceptions are made. SBP's doors are open — wide open. *60 Minutes* presented the case of a student who showed up at the school's pool one day and told the swimming coach that he had no place to live and wanted to play water polo. The coach, following his innate kindness and the Benedictine Rule, told the boy to come to the school prepared to play water polo and to live in the Leahy House.

A large part of Father Ed's success is due to the fact that he has made counseling a central element at SBP. Of the 550 students, 200 are in regular counseling either on a one-on-one basis or in groups. When you understand the boys' backgrounds, you understand why counseling is vital to their success. The counseling program is divided into four groups: substance abuse, depression (called "Blues Brothers"), unknown sons (absent dads or fractured relationships with their fathers), and anger management. SBP counselors are active, widely known, and operate with an open door policy.

I was brought to tears several times during my visit hearing the stories of some of the students. Many don't know their mothers, some were raised in foster homes, and others come from homes where drugs and alcohol rule the day. Some of the boys were homeless before SBP found them or they found SBP.

After our personal interview, Father Ed asked if I wanted a tour of the school. Eager to see more, I immediately said yes, and he summoned a sophomore whom I recognized from the *60 Minutes* piece to guide me. During the tour, I noticed that students knew one another by name. One of SBP's mottos is "Whatever hurts my brother hurts me."

In a city where the public school drop-out rate is 30%, 98% of SBP seniors graduate and 87% of them go on to earn college degrees.

Once the freshman class is formed, all the students are required to go on a five-day, 55 mile hike on the Appalachian Trail. This is a bonding experience meant to form camaraderie among the boys and fill them with self-confidence. The "you can do it" feeling is ever present at SBP.

The school is a cloistered environment, encouraging students, teachers, and monks to develop close relationships with one another. Creating community is a priority, as is accepting yourself, your life, and your history. A "You are only as sick as your secrets" philosophy and the intense counseling allows secrets to be divulged and dealt with as completely as possible.

St. Benedict's Prep is a shinning example of what love can do — of the magic of caring and making students feel that they matter. Time and again in our lives, we experience the presence or the absence of love and feel the difference it makes. Father Ed, his staff, and the students are prime examples of what can be achieved through love and the power of three simple, but profound words "You are loved."

To watch the 60 Minutes segment, please go to www.sbp.org/60Minutes.

SHAWN RUX

I recently read an article about a New York City public school principal who has been performing miracles in a school that had a grade of "F" prior to his appointment. In 2011, the Board of Education appointed Shawn Rux principal of the much-troubled Middle School 53 Brian Piccolo in Queens, New York. On paper, this was a mission impossible type of school with a well established climate of failure, but through the leadership and innovation of this dynamic man, the unraveling, deficient school soon turned the "F" into a glowing passing grade.

I met Shawn Rux in his office during the Christmas Holidays, a few days before New Year's Eve. Not only was he at work, but it was a regular working day for him although the students and teachers were all on break. It turns out, Principal Rux is at the school practically every day. As he greeted me, I could feel his pride in showing me what MS 53 had become under his leadership. He clearly had ownership of the school in the best sense of the word.

Rux was wearing a long-sleeved sweatshirt bearing the logo **MS 53, Education Saves Lives** in bold letters. His smile and positive attitude showed him as a living example of that and of what can happen to a failing school when a caring, qualified professional is given the reins.

MS 53 has a student population of 365 ten to fourteen year olds in grades 6, 7, and 8. Before Rux arrived, the school averaged 280 suspensions a year, but since he took over the number has dropped to fewer than 40. He doesn't believe in suspending students because a suspension only means that the student will miss precious school days. Besides, the school's present climate of peace and order discourages behavior leading to suspension. Daily attendance is up, approaching 90%, which indicates that students want to attend this school, once a pariah of the New York City public school system.

MS 53 is located in Far Rockaway, an area hit hard two years earlier by a hurricane. The school is around 3 miles from where Rux and his family live. When he first got the appointment, he used to drive 3 hours from New Jersey, but soon realized that a move was in order. In fact, he jokes that he now lives a short bike ride away.

Mr. Rux personally greets the students every morning at the front entrance — he knows most of them by name. He has also implemented a number of strategies that cost the New York City Board of Education nothing in terms of dollars, but have proven extremely effective in turning around the school. For example, MS 53 now keeps all grade levels on separate floors with classes and lunch periods separated by gender. Rux explains that, at that age, children are very conscious of the opposite sex and, as a result, do not perform as well academically when classes are mixed. In being separated by gender, students are less self-conscious about their bodies and clothing and more open towards academics. Students have proven to be more productive this way. This small change in class structure has made a big difference in the overall climate of the school.

When asked how many children he has, Rux quickly responds 365 followed by a knowing smile, and he means it. One quickly picks up on this man's genuineness. He is charismatic and loves the work he does, the success he has achieved, and all the children in his school, no exceptions. He says he was greatly influenced by his 4th grade teacher who made him feel special and now he strives to pass along that same feeling to his students at MS 53.

The school's difference and specialness recently caught the attention of *The Today Show* on NBC. The show featured Shawn Rux in a segment hosted by Sheinelle Jones. A section of the piece shows him doing a hip-hop dance extolling the merits of the school and his students. Yes, principal Rux does a good hip-hop! Ms. Jones also interviewed a school janitor who has worked at MS 53 since 1978. He talked about the positive difference Shawn Rux has made in the lives of students and the staff. What was once chaotic is now a joyful place of order and productivity.

While in Shawn's office, I noticed a poster of Nelson Mandela with a quotation that read: *Education is the most powerful weapon which you can use to change the world.* The poster also had an inscription that read: MS 53 Brian Piccolo salutes Nelson Mandela (1918-2013). There were also several Superman figurines around the office because Shawn has been fascinated since childhood by the concept of Superman; someone dedicated to helping others.

When asked what qualities he feels he has brought to MS 53, Shawn mentions passion, seriousness, love for kids and education, collaboration, opportunity, hope, and SWAGGER. He defines *SWAGGER* as *S*tudents *W*ho *A*chieve *G*ood *G*rades *E*arn *R*espect. MS 53 students know the meaning of SWAGGER.

A big part of the school's success comes from Rux's way of selecting his faculty. During the interview process, in addition to being academically sound, candidates must somehow prove that they love children. Love of children is an essential element of his evaluation process.

Shawn Rux wants to have a global impact on children. He has already begun the process at MS 53. The question now is, if he can so successfully turn around an "F" rated school, why can't other teachers and administrators do the same? Let Principal Rux be a beacon of light and hope for all the schools struggling in darkness.

THE VALUE OF NUTRITION: DR. JOSEPH DEL GIODICE & CHEF TONI'S COOKING ADVENTURES

One of the ways we can influence and improve the life of our students is through the food we serve them in school cafeterias. Several studies have shown the amazing results of feeding vegan diets to prison inmates, and even though students are not prisoners, they are nevertheless inmates of a sort since they spend six or more hours at school on a daily basis. Students are a captive audience, so let us make certain we serve them clean, healthy food — currently, the food is neither. While students are inside school walls, we should guarantee a climate that supports both mental and physical health, and providing them with healthy, nourishing food with little or no sugar added would go a long way toward accomplishing this goal.

Many schools routinely keep soda and candy machines available for students to purchase all sorts of junk food whenever they wish. How about demanding that these machines be removed from school property? Junk food is filled with sugar and sugar is a poison responsible for the weight gain epidemic currently attacking our youth and for acidic body conditions that contribute to cancers and diabetes.

I consulted Dr. Joseph Del Giodice, a noted naturopathic physician, on the topic of nutrition in schools. Dr. Del Giodice shared the following:

"When considering the state of our children's educational wellbeing, I begin in the kitchen. Some may wonder what this one room of the house has to do with scholastic achievement. My answer is that the brain only functions as well as the quality of the fuel we provide it. Let's think for a moment about a big performance automobile engine. We could perhaps drive for a while on low octane, low quality, diluted fuel, but very soon the way the engine runs becomes compromised, it misfires, hesitates during acceleration, has reduced fuel economy, produces greater pollutants, and ultimately has a shortened lifespan.

In modern times, with fast foods, junk foods, and highly refined chemically laden foods, far too many of our children are overfed and under-nourished. When this happens, the brain and the emotional well being ultimately suffer. The mass production used in today's fast and packaged foods provide a steady stream of chemicals that disrupt blood sugar levels (the neurons in the brain run on glucose), introduce proven neurotoxins, and promote dehydration (the brain needs abundant hydration to function properly). Any basic level textbook on human nutrition tells us all the nutrients required for brain and emotional health. These nutrients are not abundant in a diet of frozen microwave snacks, brightly colored artificial sweet drinks, candies, deep fried chips, and chemical sugar substitutes. The good news is that these crucial nutrients — B Vitamins, amino acids, macro and micro minerals, pure hydration, complex carbohydrates, enzymes and co-enzymes, and essential fatty acids — are abundant in a plant focused diet that has fresh vegetables and fruits of all colors, clean proteins, and natural unrefined sources of high quality fat.

Given that the human brain, particularly the brain of a growing child, is far more complex than any automobile engine, computer, or piece of intricate machinery, any model of educational planning must include these very basic and common sense principles of health and nutrition. The bodies, brains, emotional health, and ultimately the future of our most precious resource, i.e. our children, depend on it."

It is my opinion that our Standard American Diet (SAD) will only be successfully substituted with healthy eating if we begin with the children. Our hope for a culture of healthy eating lies with our children.

While watching a news show, I came across an interesting interview on FOX 5 in the New York City market. Rosanna Scotto and Greg Kelly were interviewing Antoinette Willard, also known as Chef Toni, who owns a business called *Chef Toni's Cooking Adventures: Cook, Eat & Play with Love*. Chef Toni and her partner, Inna Sobel, run several cooking schools for children ages 3 to 13 in New York City. Their goal is to teach children about good, clean food and nutritious eating habits.

I visited Chef Toni's cooking school on the Upper West Side of Manhattan and found her to be enthusiastic, full of love toward the children, and passionate about her work with food. Being in her company was pure joy. Chef Toni graciously sat for an interview along with her business partner, Inna Sobel, who takes care of the business side of things and is equally enthusiastic about the work they perform.

Chef Toni and Ms. Sobel are proud to say that their school, in addition to cooking, also teaches a variety of life skills, instills confidence in children, allows them to learn how to follow directions, promotes good eating habits, and shows the importance of time management.

Chef Toni's cooking school came about in a most interesting manner. Her own child did not enjoy the food being served at a public school in New York City. As a result, Chef Toni joined the school's PTA, became its vice-president, and got involved with the school's food choices. She then started an after-school program to teach kids how to cook and how to appreciate what they were eating. The program began twelve years ago with a handful of children and now its five campuses in Manhattan operate with a long waiting list of those who yearn to be part of the program. While the interview was taking place, an enthusiastic seven year old boy came up to Chef Toni and asked if he could cook something. He asked with the enthusiasm of an inspired boy and that impressed me.

On the subject of how the students are treated, Chef Toni said, "I think the attention we give the kids gives them confidence and independence." Ms. Sobel added, "The program changes the way kids eat and think about eating."

Chef Toni's Cooking Adventures welcomes both public and private school stunts. They teach different ethnic foods along with background on the culture l country being spotlighted. Knife skills are also part of the curriculum.

Why can't we teach cooking and food appreciation to all public school chil-

Granted, most high schools offer a Home Economics class that is virtually

a cooking class, but we could begin this process much earlier so that good cooking and a full understanding of food and nutrition is taught to students beginning in Kindergarten. If we did it Chef Toni's way, it could be accomplished.

VISITACIÓN VALLEY
MIDDLE SCHOOL

There is a middle school in the San Francisco Bay Area that uses a new idea called *Quiet Time* on a daily basis. The Visitación Valley Middle School sounds a gong twice a day and even rowdy adolescents sit still, shut their eyes, clear their minds, and meditate. Professor David Kirp from the University of California in Berkeley wrote an article on the *Quiet Time* at the Visitación Valley Middle School in which he states that the results are quite impressive.

As the professor discovered, this is meditation rebranded and it deserves serious attention from parents and school administrators all over the country. An array of studies have shown that meditation during the school day has a positive effect on student behavior and academic performance.[56]

In 2007, Visitación Valley Middle School became the first public school to adopt the program. The sound of gunfire is common in that neighborhood and there were nine shootings in the nine months preceding the professor's article. Most of the students in the school know someone who has been shot or who has done the shooting. Murders are so frequent that the school employs a full-time grief counselor.

The *Quiet Time* has made all the difference inside the school. Students who were largely out of control before this meditative practice, with absenteeism rates among the city's highest, with worn-out teachers, can now enjoy a climate of peace and achievement.

In the first year of *Quiet Time*, student suspensions fell by 45%. After four years of the program, the suspension rate was among the lowest among area schools and daily attendance climbed to 98%. There was even a test administered that measured the students' happiness level and *Quiet Time* students were at the top. Three other schools in the area adopted the program and their positive scores increased as well.

Something as simple as meditation twice a day turned a troubled school into a model school. Why can't other districts try *Quiet Time* or something of that order? It costs the Board of Education nothing in terms of money, but pays a fortune in positive results. Our energy changes when we meditate and changing the energy of misbehaving students sounds worthy of a try.

Yoga could also be added to public school gym classes. I have seen first hand how yoga quiets the mind and stills the body. The results of a yoga practice would be wonderful for students and would cost schools nothing. I have always been amazed at the way that schools' gym classes concentrate on teaching basketball, baseball, and football when students entering the professional ranks in those sports make up a fraction of a decimal point. The practice of yoga, on the other hand, can make for a lifetime of healthy body-mind exercises in addition to being one of the best strategies for stress reduction and relaxation.

I am also an advocate of teaching social dancing in gym classes. Dancing teaches grace, coordination, rhythm, and social interaction with the opposite sex. It would give children confidence in attending school dances and social events for the rest of their lives. Furthermore, I urge schools to place more emphasis on more practical life sports like tennis, golf, and hiking.

FOOTNOTES

[1] New York Post 8/4/15

[2] WSJ Saturday/Sunday September 27-28, 2014, page A17

[3] Ray Kerrison, *New York Post*, December 21, 1997.

[4] *Public Agenda*, "Getting By: What American Teenagers Really Think About Their Schools," 1997, p. 35.

[5] "Getting By," p. 36.

[6] "Getting By," p. 36.

[7] "Getting By," p. 36.

[8] "Getting By," p. 36.

[9] Teaching Community, *Survey Reveals What Students Really Think of Teachers* November 19, 2008.

[10] *Public Agenda*, "Given The Circumstances: Teachers Talk About Public Education Today," 1996, p. 11.

[11] "Given The Circumstances," p. 12.

[12] "Given The Circumstances," p. 12.

[13] US News and World Report, April 9, 2014

[14] "Given The Circumstances," p. 13.

[15] "Given The Circumstances," p. 13.

[16] PEPG Survey, *What Americans Think About Their Schools* Fall 2007, Vol. 7, No. 4, Fall 2007.

[17] *StateImpact*, March 8, 2012.

[18] *Education Week*, March 14, 2012.

[19] "Assignment Incomplete," p. 31.

[20] *Education Week*, Vol. XVII, Number 17, January 8, 1998.

[21] PEPG *What Americans Think About Their Schools*, Vol. 7, No. 4

[22] Professor Rosetta Marantz Cohen, Smith College, *Insight* published September 9, 2013.

Education Week, pp. 10-12.

Education Week, p. 10.

Education Week, pp. 10-12.

26 *Public Agenda, Are We Beginning to See the Light?* 2010

27 Lyndsey Layton, *The Washington Post,* January 16, 2015

28 Assignment Incomplete, p. 13.

29 Public Agenda, June 2, 2010, *Are We Beginning to See The Light?*

30 "Assignment Incomplete," pp. 13-14.

31 *New York Post,* December 21, 1997, pp. 8-9.

32 *The New York Times,* Sunday, February 21, 1999

33 *Public Agenda,* "First Things First," p. 37.

34 *What Americans Think about Their Schools,* Fall 2007, Vol. 7, No. 4, PEPG Survey

35 *Public Agenda, Are We Beginning to See the Light?,* June 2010

36 April 29, 2014, *Teachers Versus the Public: What Americans think about Schools and How to Fix Them*

37 *Time,* October 27, 1997, p. 96.

38 *Public Agenda,* "Different Drummers: How Teachers of Teachers View Public Education," 1997, p. 17.

39 "Different Drummers," p. 18.

40 Ralph Waldo Emerson, "Letters and Social Aims," 1876.

41 Ray Kerrison, New York Post, December 21, 1997.

42 Dr. Wollerstein, as mentioned by Dr. James Dobson on *Focus On The Family* radio broadcast.

43 Tennessee Williams, transcript of a personal television interview, *The David FrostShow* (January 21, 1970), p. 8.

44 Dr. James C. Dobson, *Home With A Heart,* Tyndale House Publishers, Inc., Wheaton Illinois, 1996, p. 164.

45 "Dear Abby" advice column, nationally syndicated newspaper feature.

46 *New York Post,* November 16, 1997, p 9.

47 *Public Agenda,* "Getting By," p. 28.

48 *Public Agenda,* "Getting By," p. 28.

49 William Shakespeare, *Macbeth,* Act IV, Scene 2, lines 73-76.

50 *Public Agenda,* "First Things First: What Americans Expect From The Public Schools," 1994, p. 10.

51 *Public Agenda,* "First Things First," p. 10.

52 WSJ Sat. Sun., Dec. 7-8, 2013, p. C1, Lee Siegel

[53] *Public Agenda*, "Kids These Days: What Americans Really Think About The Next Generation," 1997, p. 8.

[54] *Public Agenda*, "Kids These Days," p. 23.

[55] *Public Agenda*, "Kids These Days," p. 23.

[56] Professor David Kirp, January 12, 2014, SFGate.